HAUNTED

YORKSHIRE DALES

HAUNTED
YORKSHIRE
DALES

Summer Strevens

The
History
Press

With grateful thanks to the endless list of those generous souls of the Yorkshire Dales, who have shared their time and experiences with unreserved enthusiasm to help me write this book; their spirit and strength of character are the fabric of the Dales.

First published 2011

The History Press
The Mill, Brimscombe Port
Stroud, Gloucestershire, GL5 2QG
www.thehistorypress.co.uk

© Summer Strevens, 2011

The right of Summer Strevens to be identified as the Author
of this work has been asserted in accordance with the
Copyrights, Designs and Patents Act 1988.

British Library Cataloguing in Publication Data.
A catalogue record for this book is available from the British Library.

ISBN 978 0 7524 5887 8
Typesetting and origination by The History Press
Printed in Great Britain
Manufacturing managed by Jellyfish Print Solutions Ltd

Contents

Introduction

MUCH has been written about the beauty of the Yorkshire Dales; this designated Area of Outstanding Natural Beauty is home and workplace to the some 20,000 people who inhabit the region, and is swelled each year by over 8 million visitors who come to marvel at this stunning part of the British Isles.

Powerful belief and superstition still hold true in the Dales, which is rich in folklore and mythology and a natural breeding ground for the many and varied tales and legends of ghosts and hauntings abounding throughout the area's history, of which I hope to give you a flavour here.

As well as shaping the collective consciousness, this vertical empire has been physically sculpted by the advancing and retreating glaciation of the last of the Ice Age, leaving a legacy of outcrops, pavements, valleys and moraine deposits that give us the characteristic view of the Dales we see today. Displays of steeply exposed rugged limestone crags contrast with the lower slopes where criss-cross networks of dry-stone walls, each yard comprising of some ton and a half of stone, draw the eye towards lush, glaciated river valleys. In the summer months, livestock thrive in the pastures dotted with stone barns and where waterfalls thunder after heavy rain. The remarkable geology of the Dales is further enhanced by the hand of man with the construction of fortifications, monastic houses, bridges, towns and villages along with the scars of the Dale's industrial history also apparent in the landscape, yet each Dale has its own distinctive character, as captured in the lines of Dales author Alfred J. Brown:

> One of the charms of the Yorkshire Dales is that they are all characteristically different, like the lovely sisters of the same family. Each Dale has its distinctive features, folklore and legends, and each must be explored from end to end if one wishes to understand its fame and beauty.

As to Dales folk themselves, the combined Yorkshire memory is elephantine, and in spite of their 'no nonsense' approach to life, the need to reinforce explanations for the unexplained is an irresistible urge exhibited throughout the collective folk memory. Many of the accounts appearing in this book have been set down in print before, while some have been freshly brought to light through research and investigation; some stem back hundreds of years, others are relatively modern, born from the continuing oral tradition for reiterating stories in the age-old fashion. However, all are genuinely held accounts of hauntings from the other side.

In compiling these haunting tales from the Yorkshire Dales, I have employed the 'classical' definition of the Dales region encompassing the Yorkshire Dales National Park and areas of the Nidderdale and North Pennine Areas of Outstanding Natural Beauty. While some of the towns and villages mentioned are on the fringes of these boundaries, I hope the reader will forgive me if I have strayed slightly to include the odd tale from a location not strictly adhering to these borders as, in these cases, exclusion on a point of strict geographical stricture would rob the reader of some tales worthy of inclusion with the others.

In addition to the accounts of ghostly goings-on, I hope to provide an historical background and basis for the sightings herein, and a feel for both the popular and sometimes lesser-known places all over the Dales where varied instances of apparitions from the afterlife have been known to occur. And rather than use the tried (or tired) and tested method of plotting each haunting by location, I have opted to categorise each chapter thematically by style of haunting as opposed to confining them by district, hopefully providing a more varied and enjoyable read.

Whether you live in the Dales, are a visitor to the area or just plain interested in the unexplained, I hope you will enjoy these haunting tales from the Yorkshire Dales as much as I have enjoyed researching and writing about them.

Unless otherwise stated, all of the photographs featured in this book are copyright of Jack Gritton, 2011.

Summer Strevens, 2011
www.hauntedyorkshiredales.co.uk

1.

Ladies In Black

A popular apparition in the North Yorkshire Dales, tales of ghostly black-clad ladies seem to proliferate more than any other kind of manifestation, with the odd sprinkling of grey and even blue ladies thrown in for good measure.

Our first Lady in Black favours a 200-yard stretch of the road between Aysgarth and Woodhall. Although well known in the district there is no local legend to account for her appearances, in spite of the fact that her dress would indicate that (in haunting terms) she is a fairly recent addition. Variously described as mid-Victorian wearing a crinolined black dress, coloured bonnet and white gloves, this Black Lady also carries a walking stick, and while several people have addressed her mistaking her for someone living, she never replies.

Coverham church and surrounding Middleham Low Moor also lay claim to a Black Lady, who apparently rises from the churchyard of the lonely and now redundant Holy Trinity, located close to the site of the twelfth-century Premonstratensian Abbey at Coverham. The abbey was famous before the Dissolution for the White Monks with their superb singing voices and the equally superb white horses that the brothers bred. Setting off from the church in the direction of the moor, the regular apparition, clothed in a long black mourning coat vanishes at her habitual dematerialisation point at 'Courting' Wall Corner, so named as this was a favourite meeting place for young lovers, though obviously a corruption of 'Cotescue' Wall Corner as the location now appears on modern maps, and associated with the rather fine eighteenth-century Cotescue Park, a country house in close proximity to our haunting and possibly her former home.

Famed for her extraordinary beauty and of good local family, the Lady in Black is said to have been paid court by many suitors, but after finally narrowing her choice to one lucky chap from a shortlist whittled down to two rival lovers, the spurned party committed a crime passionnel after failing to coerce the object of his affections into a change of heart. Strangled by her thwarted lover at Courting Wall Corner, the incidence of her appearances were said to decrease somewhat after the discovery made by peat cutters working on the moor in the early 1900s of a female skeleton with tattered remains of black cloth attached. However, a more recent firm sighting of this Black Lady was made by a shaken cyclist in the winter of 1993, although before that her lone progress had concerned other motorists who similarly experienced her inexplicable evaporation. An equally mysterious black-clad female is said to have opened a gate for some walkers in the vicinity, her subsequent disappearance engendering a likewise unnerving experience in this beautiful but oft-times desolate location.

Now a lady with more solid provenance, Mary Queen of Scots, who can lay serious claim to perhaps the busiest manifestation in the British Isles.

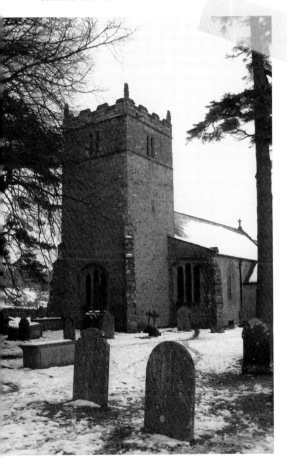

Coverham church, setting for the Black Lady's materialisation.

She is said to haunt Nappa Hall near Askrigg, just down the road from our first apparition on the Aysgarth-Woodhall road.

Attired in black velvet, a spectral woman with a beautiful face (coincidentally looking very much like contemporary portraits of Mary) is supposed to haunt this fifteenth-century fortified manner house, the chief seat of the Metcalfes in Wensleydale which, next to Bolton Castle, is the most important of the ancient homesteads in the Dales. A vivid account of the apparition was written down by a visitor to the Hall in 1878:

> I was in the hall playing hide and seek with the farmer's daughter, a child of about 4 years old. The hall was dimly lit by a fire and a candle in a room in the east tower. Whilst we played, someone entered the hall from the lower end, and walked towards [the] dais. Thinking it was the farmer's wife, I ran after her and was going to touch her, when she turned around and I saw her face. It was lovely and her dress seemed to be made of black velvet. After looking at me for a moment, she went on and disappeared through the door to the winding stone staircase in the direction of the turret of the west tower. Her face, figure and general appearance reminded me of portraits of Mary Queen of Scots.

Mary stayed at Nappa in 1568 as a respite to her period of confinement at nearby Bolton Castle, although 'confinement' may conjure up too harsh a picture of her constraint at that point, as at that time Mary had fifty-one personal servants attending her. Not surprisingly, she has also been known to put in an appearance at Bolton Castle itself, favouring the courtyard, although she has also been spotted in the castle chapel and outside the castle walls on at least two occasions.

Bolton Castle, spectacular mediaeval fortress preserved in outstanding condition, situated in the heart of Wensleydale.

The haunting Semerwater.

Moving on now to Gunnerside in Swaledale, described as a 'woman' in black (perhaps her dress is not as classy as the Queen of Scots' velvet) this haunting occurs at Gunnerside Lodge on stormy nights and is said to be the unfortunate result of a fire tragically claiming her life. Situated on the west side of Shore Gill, the extensive buildings of Gunnerside Lodge look down on the tiny hamlet of Ivelet, so perhaps the unfortunate lady had an encounter with that famous portent of tragedy – the phantom headless hound of Ivelet Bridge? (We shall be visiting the topic of ghostly hounds in a later chapter.)

Still with ghostly women in dresses, although in this instance we have no descriptive colour, a female form is said to lurk about Countersett Hall at Semerwater, which in the seventeenth century was the dwelling of Richard Robinson, the first Quaker in Wensleydale. Little more is known of our colourless ghost, although folklorist Edmund Bogg noted in his *A thousand miles in the Valleys of the Nidd and Yore*, first published in 1894, that 'a rough road from Bainbridge to the north side of the lake passes Semmerdale Hall, where the Dale's folk say that on dark nights ghosts, arrayed in white apparel, are still to be seen wandering.' Semmerdale Hall is a close neighbour of Countersett Hall, less than half a mile along the rough road described by Bogg, and perhaps these white-clad apparitions and our lady ghost are connected with the local legend of a vanished town in the vicinity. It is said that a beggar once came to the town asking for shelter, but after being turned away at every door he eventually came to a farm on the nearby hillside where a kindly old couple let him in. Next morning the beggar had gone, but the whole town excepting the poor old couple's cottage had been punished for its lack of charity by being completely submerged underwater, now known as Semerwater and North Yorkshire's largest natural lake. Some believe that the beggar was actually an angel sent to test the goodness of the townsfolk renowned for their selfishness and greed, and on finding them wholly wanting chanted:

Semerwater rise! Semerwater sink!
And swallow the town, all save this house,
Where they gave me meat and drink.

Some even say that the old church bells can be heard ringing underwater and that occasionally buildings can be seen at the bottom of the lake. On a path leading from the southern lake shore is the now romantically ruined old chapel to the tiny hamlet of Stalling Busk, although the churchyard is still used for burials. Though the exact location of her haunting is unknown, a Grey Lady is supposed to frequent this area, and is thought to be connected to nearby Raydale House. This seventeenth-century building was largely rebuilt during the nineteenth century, at which time it acquired a reputation for being haunted. Possibly the renovation work had disturbed those who lost their lives in the siege laid against the house in 1617, which was generated by a feud between Thomas Metcalfe and the then owners of the Hall, the Robinsons. Raydale House has also been subject to the unseen but all too audible phantom of a galloping horseman heard to approach the house in the dead of night, dismount and bang on the door. He is conspicuous in his absence when the door is answered, coupled with a distinct absence of hoof-prints. Another noisy ghostly occupant of Raydale, referred to as 'Auld Opper', was noted by Edmund Bogg in his writings about the area when he recorded that:

> One elderly woman told us, with all seriousness, that in her young days she dwelt there, and the ghost from its unearthly knocking on the various articles of furniture was a source of continual terror. This woman had not only heard Auld 'Opper knock, but actually had seen him, she said, 'mony a time'. Unfortunately we did not think to enquire in what form the ghost appeared.

Clearly the Stalling Busk Grey Lady does not want for spectral company.

While not entirely grey, but described as wearing a grey cloak, the ghost of the infanticidal Nanny Trotter has been seen at Pinska Gill, or Pinskey Gill in the modern spelling, where she drowned her illegitimate child in the secluded rivulet near Ravonstonedale on the border of the Dales with Cumbria. In spite of passing the spot at various times and in various weathers, the Revd W. Nicholls, author of *The History and Traditions of Ravenstonedale,* published in 1877, failed to make a positive sighting, perhaps denying him the opportunity of 'laying' the spirit of Nanny once and for all.

Another Grey Lady proper is said to put in a appearance in the graveyard of

The churchyard of St Michael the Archangel, Kirkby Malham.

The now ruined battlements of Barnard Castle, perched above the River Tees.

St Michael the Archangel at Kirkby Malham. Termed as the 'Cathedral of the Dales', the austerely beautiful fifteenth-century St Michael's, whose bells incidentally are heard by Tom in Charles Kingsley's *Water Babies*, is naturally a draw for tourists, responsible for numerous sightings of this monochrome manifestation and in good company with the many inhabitants of the village who have also seen her emerging from the side of a smashed grave. The grave has now been repaired, possibly inhibit-ing this Grey Lady's egress into the realm of the living. Perhaps in life she was foolish enough to partake in the Malhamdale 'banquet of the dead', a lavish feast set out by the Devil in the graveyard of St Michael's once a year at midnight and designed to lure the living to him. Thankfully, the last person to sit down to such a devilish dinner was the village parson, who was clever enough to banish the Devil by asking him for some salt.

From austere churches to imposing ruins, where there resides an apparition of no specific recorded hue, so we must perhaps assume her transparent. Lady Ann Day occasionally re-enacts the violent plummet to her death from the walls of Barnard Castle, the now ruined twelfth-century bastion perched high on a cliff overlooking the River Tees and giving rise to the town's name. Lady Ann was pushed by an unknown assailant from the castle ramparts in the reign of Queen Mary, and perhaps understandably Lady Ann's ghost also makes an audible contribution and can be heard wailing and bemoaning her tragic fate as she falls to her watery grave.

Moving to the lighter end of the haunting spectrum, a trio of White Ladies. The first unidentified apparition puts in an appearance at the Bluebell Hotel in Kettlewell, where, despite a particular penchant for frequenting the laundry room, she likes nothing better than to drift around the bedrooms of this popular inn, dating from around 1680. Our second alabaster apparition, most active around sunset on a winter's evening, is the White Lady who frequents Flood Lane, an area famous for its colourful profusion of wild flowers and the road linking the river bridges at either end of Dent, the beautiful town with cobbled streets from which the valley of Dentdale derives its name. Appearing when the lane is awash with flood water from the River Dee, habitually spilling onto the road after heavy rain, tradition holds that this unfortunate wraith was taking victuals to her husband who was working in a field nearby, but, on finding him injured, she was tragically swept away by the swollen river torrent as she hurriedly went for help. If seen, however, she vanishes immediately. Nothing firm is known of the background to the third white lady, who haunts High Clapdale Farm near Clapham, although she may well be associated with accused witch Alice Kyteler (see Chapter 9 for more about this lady and her satanic associations). Her regular late evening appearances were most numerously reported by visiting students (staying at the farm when on lease to the University of Lancaster) and perhaps offering a 'sobering' experience!

Finally, a couple of flashes of colour from a pair of 'Blue Ladies'. The first Catherine Parr, holding the distinction of sixth and last wife of Henry VIII, she is said to emanate a sense of serenity whenever she has appeared dressed in blue at Snape Castle, located in the village of the same name close to Beadale and the nearby beautifully laid out arboretum at Thorp Perrow. Home to one of the finest private collections of trees and shrubs in the country, Thorp Perrow boasts amongst its many impressive specimens from the sixteenth and seventeenth centuries the romantically named 'Catherine Parr's Oak'. Catherine resided for some years at Snape when married to its owner and her then second husband John Neville, the third Lord Latimer. Perhaps this accounts for her tranquil countenance radiating peace and calm, as this union preceded her unlooked for marital obligation to the increasingly overweight, tyrannical and somewhat cranky Henry. (As a point of interest, Catherine's ghost has taken on a greenish tinge in the haunting of her final residence at Sudeley Castle in Gloucestershire.)

Our last lady may be blue for a reason, as the daughter of Sir Stephen Proctor was said to have been 'cruelly done to death' at Fountains Hall near Ripon. Apparently witness to her father's evil doings (Proctor's use of the abbey ruins as a free and pre-quarried supply of building material for the construction of the Hall met strong disapproval from his daughter), Fountains Hall was completed in 1604. But it is said that the spirit of the Blue Lady will remain at the Hall for all eternity in an attempt to deter visitors entering her one-time home, in her eyes the product of paternal profanity. Incidentally, Fountains Hall plays host to another ghosts, namely an unidentified, ruff-wearing Elizabethan man who has been seen to emerge from the panelling in front of a solid stone wall, so perhaps this Blue Lady has some company in her eternal deterring vigil after all.

So, remember to keep an eye out for any unusually hued ghostly ladies; you could earn your slice of fame – the annals still have room for polka dots!

Snape Castle, one-time home to Henry VIII's sixth and last queen.

Fountains Hall, residence in perpetuity to the Blue Lady.

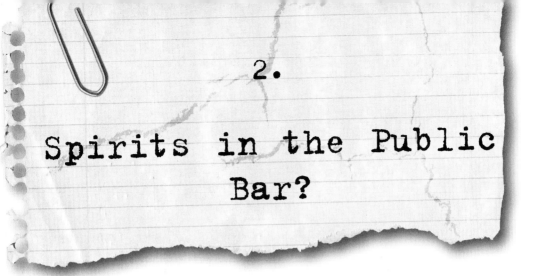

2.

Spirits in the Public Bar?

EVERYONE must be familiar with the old adage that every public house in the country can boast the presence of at least one spirit if you count the contents of the top shelf, but there are many hostelries in the Yorkshire Dales boasting rather more than the bottled variety.

As mentioned in the chapter covering 'Ecclesiastic Ectoplasm', a brace of monks are known to haunt two of the public houses in the Wensleydale district, with monastic manifestations at The Fox & Hounds in West Witton and the Palmer Flatt Hotel at Aysgarth, but let us begin our spectral pub crawl in the old city of Ripon, where the Unicorn Hotel offers an unusual but friendly spectre in the shape of 'Old Boots'.

The bustling market town of Ripon was founded over 1,300 years ago and is famed for the beautiful cathedral begun by St Wilfrid in AD 672, for the unbroken 1,000-year-old tradition of the Wakeman sounding his horn every evening (*see* 'Ghostly Sounds' for more about the Wakeman's spectral appearances) and the unusual but friendly spectre of 'Old

Boots' who frequents the Unicorn Hotel facing on to the main square.

Along with the Black Bull, the Unicorn was one of the primary stop-over for many

The Unicorn Hotel, facing Ripon's famous Market Square and obelisk commemorating the 1,000-year-old tradition of the Wakeman's Horn.

stagecoaches running between Newcastle, Leeds and London, as well as the focal destination for many local carriage companies making a change of horse. Verified by historical poll tax returns, the Unicorn has been in the business of selling beer since 1379; however, in the haunting scheme of things, Old Boots seems to have been a more recent addition as his employ with the inn dates to several decades from the 1760s. To give him his real name, Tom Crudd, also known as Thomas Spence, was a servant at the Unicorn Hotel and was responsible for assisting arriving weary travellers with the removal of their boots, and usually introduced himself with a pair of slippers in one hand and a boot jack in the other, hence his nickname. However, Tom was clever enough to supplement his wage by making play of his extraordinary appearance, namely an enormous nose and chin. Thanks to these facial abnormalities, (one imagines comparable to Mr Punch) Tom was able to acquire extra tips by demonstrating how he could hold a coin in between nose and chin, cannily keeping hold of the money as payment for his performance. Old Boots' non-frightening ghost is still said to haunt the hotel but it's not known if he still performs his pecuniary party piece.

Moving on to another Unicorn, this time the Ancient Unicorn in Bowes. (In the late middle ages, with widespread illiteracy and when inns were required to display an easily recognisable sign, many hostlers opted for animal symbols, and the Unicorn's association with ferocity and strength, coupled with the belief that drinking from a unicorn cup guarded against poison, made it a popular choice of name, presumably the latter symbolism holding no inference as to the quality of the beer served in an inn under such a sign!) As a coaching inn, the Ancient Unicorn can trace its history back to the sixteenth century when the Stainmore Pass (now the A66) was an important trade route. As well as the ghosts of a twelve-year-old boy frequenting the cellars (he'd been thrown down there as a punishment and not allowed back out ever again) and a woman described as wearing a grey 'smock-like' Victorian dress, the Ancient Unicorn is also the haunt of 'Edwin and Emma', tragic lovers whose story was poetically immortalised in the ballad the 'Bowes Tragedy'.

Edwin and Emma (or Roger Wrightson and Martha Ritson to give them their real names) were both from inn-keeping families (Roger's kept the Kings' Head – no longer in existence – and Martha's family the Unicorn). The couple fell in love in 1713, but the match faced parental hostility, Roger's family feeling they were a cut above the Ritsons, thus necessitating the lovers meeting in secret. Their year-long hidden romance was cut short when Roger fell seriously ill with fever on Shrove Tuesday 1714. As Roger neared death, his parents relented and allowed Martha to see her love one last time, Roger dying three days later. Martha in her turn died shortly afterwards, it is said from a broken heart, but the two were ultimately united as they were buried together at the west end of St Giles' churchyard, and rising from this shared grave the ghosts of 'Edwin and Emma' have regularly been seen haunting the Ancient Unicorn.

A few miles from Bowes in Barnard Castle, affectionately known as 'Barney' to those who live in this historic, thriving market town we find the Old Well Inn. It is a stone's throw from the Buttermarket, the octagonal two-storied Market Cross, built in 1747, which over the years has housed a diversity of municipal functions from court, jail, Town Hall and fire station, as well as a butter market from which it takes its name

The Ancient Unicorn, Bowes, haunt of Edwin and Emma.

(the edifice now serves as a traffic roundabout!). Beer was originally brewed on the premises of the distinctive seventeenth-century inn, water conveniently supplied from the on site well – no need for exhaustive investigation into the naming of this tavern then! Noted for the manifestations specifically occurring in room 7, those enjoying the hospitality of the Old Well Inn report experiences ranging from guests feeling the bedclothes being pulled back in the middle of the night and then something climbing on to the bed with them (for as long as they remained there!) to waking in the night and finding a silent, staring child stood at the foot of the bed. Needless to say, some guests express an understandable preference when booking, although there are those who embrace the prospect of witnessing an unnerving nocturnal visit., and insist on staying in room 7.

There are no specific explanations for these manifestations as at the Ancient Unicorn in Bowes, but the Old Well Inn's situation lends to the idea that innumerable restless spirits must have passed this way as the inn is situated on Galgate, so named as this was the road that led to the town gallows where public hangings took place. In the past, the footprint that the current extent of the Old Well now occupies would have been regarded as ample capacity for up to five dwellings, and with the cholera outbreak in 1849 exacerbated by the overcrowded and squalid living conditions then regarded as the norm, perhaps our bed-hopping ghost may simply be wanting his equal share of the duvet.

At the Hopper Lane Hotel, Blubberhouses, the resident ghost actually occupies the on site well, which after extensive renovations has now been imaginatively converted into a glass-topped table. While the name Blubberhouses may conjure up images of the whaling industry, this couldn't be further from the truth as, derived from Old English, it means 'the houses by the bubbling springs'. Dating to the fifteenth century, this former coaching inn and farm is situated on the A59, the old Preston to Skipton turnpike, and while nobody really knows why this pub ghost should choose to manifest down the well shaft, the glass-topped table is an open invitation to curious patrons brave enough to peer down, possibly being treated to a sighting of this watery wraith.

More nocturnal bedroom antics have been experienced by guests staying at the Woolly Sheep in Skipton's Sheep Street. Here in room 3 (a favourite booking for ghost hunters), a presence has been known to pull down the bed sheets, while in the cellar a lady dressed in a pink ball gown appearing to billow on the breeze has been seen on more than one occasion.

The Wensleydale Heifer inn sign.

The Wensleydale Heifer, West Witton.

A member of staff noted that this particular Pink Lady seemed as surprised by his arrival to change a barrel as he was to find her in the cellar. Renovations raising the floor level by 6in presumably account for her footless legs, seen to pass through the floor.

Under the imaginatively drawn sign of the Wensleydale Heifer in West Witton, Wensleydale, this award winning seventeenth-century inn is renowned for the sumptuous seafood dishes served in the restaurant, and has been described as the Yorkshire Dale's 'first Boutique Hotel'. Numbering amongst the 'themed' accommodation offered by the inn is the 'James Herriot Room' as the Heifer was visited on occasion by the famous vet and author with his wife Helen. The inn is also host to some fishy goings on in the spectral department as well with the appearance of a ghostly lady dressed in 'a long, old fashioned light blue dress' seen after hours by staff near the open fireplace in the Whisky Club Lounge and walking through the dining room in the direction of the kitchens. She has been blamed for the inexplicable movements of hanging cook-

ware and any electrical problems or other strange goings on are also laid squarely at her door!

The audible presence of a rather unappealing landlady once echoed around what used to be the Bay Horse Inn at Burnt Yates. Her laughter was of a malicious rather than mirthful nature; the adulterous wife of the hen-pecked landlord at the time frequently derided her husband with colourful language. Thankfully, the publican was released from his strenuous marriage when she expired after a spell of confinement for insanity. Subsequently, the landlord of the Bay Horse married the far more amenable barmaid. However, his former wife's contemptuous laughter was not silenced, as she paid the happy couple one last visit on their wedding night. This was the final time her cruel mocking tone would be heard.

Another vocal visitation has been heard at the unusually named Whoop Hall Hotel (pronounced 'hoop') on the A65 south of Kirkby Lonsdale. This former coaching inn, built in 1618, serviced travellers on this once major route linking Leeds to Kendal

Lofty Tan Hill Inn, England's highest public house..

and the ghost of a murdered coachman has been known to emit shrieks and wails in the vicinity, though it is not known whether he participates in the hotel's popular 'murder mystery' weekends.

Onwards and upwards, to the Tan Hill Inn, which is generally recognised as being the highest inn in England at 1,732 ft (528m) above sea level. Tan Hill itself is a high point on the Pennine Way, placing it in the heart of real walking country and proving a welcome watering-hole for casual ramblers and ardent walkers alike, as well as host to the ghost of a former publican, Mrs Peacock. Mrs Peacock, or Mrs Parrington as she was when she took over the derelict Tan Hill in 1902 with her first husband, ran the isolated inn for nearly forty years, remarrying Michael Peacock after she was left widowed early on with three children. In view of the vulnerability of the inn's isolated position, the redoubtable Mrs Peacock took the precaution of keeping a loaded revolver in a handy position just behind the door of the living quarters, and is known to have fired it at least once. Therefore it comes as no surprise that her spirit still has a vested interest in the place, and she especially makes an appearance to oversee any work whenever alterations are being made!

More meddlesome than supervisory, the ghost inhabiting the Red Lion at Burnsall finds nothing more amusing than to turn off the beer taps and the icemaker in the cellars, which date to the twelfth century (the original 'one up one down' structure now forming the bar dates to the sixteenth century when the Red Lion was formerly the Ferryman's Inn). Similarly at the Old Swan, Gargrave, a resident ghost enjoys moving items around the bar. In a more useful vein, domestic assistance is offered at the Plough Inn at Wigglesworth, where the ghosts of landlady Gladys Saxton and a servant Mary Harrison, both tragically killed in a fire at the inn in 1945, have alerted guests to their presence with the plumping of pillows by invisible hands. The Plough Inn was built in the 1700s, and visitors have also reported frequent sightings of a woman in a long black dress around the upstairs hallway, and a phantom highwayman seen standing in the doorway. Perhaps either of these two manifestations were the cause in 1879 of another fatal accident at the inn, when former

The Red Lion,
Burnsall.

landlord Pickles Wolfenden died from his injuries after being thrown from his dog cart, but then if he were to come back and haunt the Plough himself he'd surely feel at home in the 'Pickles Bar', named in his honour.

At the Boars Head Inn, Long Preston (converted from stables to an inn in 1752 to better service travellers on the new turnpike road), the reputed ghost of a former landlord who hanged himself in the cellar is said to be held in abeyance by the photograph of his mother that hangs in the bar; as long as this is on display he won't come back! Another ghost associated with the Old Smithy, adjacent to Anvil House opposite the Boar's Head Inn, concerns the blacksmith Tom Cononley who was stabbed here in a stable yard brawl 100 years before the conversion of the Boars Head. Though Tom died at home in Settle eleven days after the fatal wound was inflicted, the metallic clang of hammer on anvil has been heard to resound around the environs of his former forge.

Another sad cellar tale comes to us from The Sportsman's Inn, Cowgill, the seventeenth-century country inn situated at the head of Dentdale, where a former landlord purchased an attractive female slave in the days of permissible human traffic. Abused and exploited, when it was discovered that the unfortunate woman was with child, the wicked landlord locked her in the cellar where eventual neglect led to her death, and presumably the source of the subsequent haunting wails emanating from below, though no laments have been heard since an exorcism was carried out in 1909.

A ghost who hasn't been back for a drink since the summer of 1879 was the local blacksmith at Buckden, the Wharfedale village at the entrance to Langstrothdale, prospering in the eighteenth century thanks to the lead mining industry and today a popular destination for visitors to the area in the shadow of the towering Buckden Pike soaring some 2,000ft above the village. The traditional Georgian coaching inn, the Buck Inn was the blacksmith's local, who after dropping dead of a seizure while working at his forge, re-enacted his post-work dash for a pint over a period of several weeks after his demise. While his haunting was of short

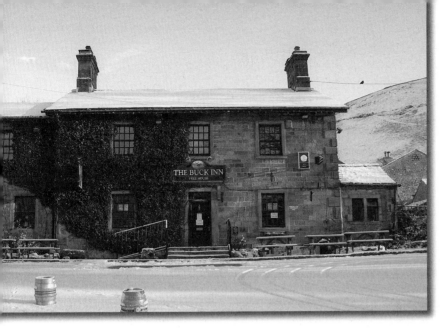

duration, each day the blacksmith's hurrying apparition would appear at the usual time, stumbling toward the hostelry entrance only to fade on entering the inn. However, the thirsty spirit was successfully laid to rest in an unusual and inventive ceremony that involved the pouring of four pints of beer onto his recently filled grave.

The Black Lion Hotel, tucked away in Richmond's Finkle Street, a side street leading from the cobbled market square, is well known for its paranormal patrons. A popular venue for haunted 'stake outs', the Georgian coaching inn is home to a plethora of phantom anomalies in the form of strange noises, orbs of light and uneasy atmospheres, with reports of people even being pushed out of the way – perhaps in an example of one type of spirit trying to obtain a measure of the other kind from the bar.

Finally, on the theme of multiple phantom occupancy, we come to a pair of Swans; the first, the Swan at Addingham, prides itself on being one of the few remaining unspoilt village alehouses in Wharfedale and boasts the ghosts of a coachman, seen

striding into the bar, a female form spotted by the fireplace, and a phantom dog (well-behaved living dogs on a lead are also

The Black Lion Hotel, Richmond. The Georgian coaching inn is home to numerous unexplained phenomona.

welcome at the Swan). At one time, the Swan was used as a mortuary (this doesn't seem to deter the locals though) and also backs on to a disused chapel (accessed through the gent's lavatory!). Popularly known today for hosting live bands, folk music and acoustic nights, the current listed building dates to the 1820s when Addingham itself was a hive of industry with a total of five operational textile mills and a large livestock market held behind the Swan. While plentiful in spirits of the ethereal variety, this has done nothing to detract from the warm and welcoming atmosphere of open fires and original features.

Where the edge of the Dales meets the wild fells of Cumbria in the unspoilt village of Ravenstonedale, named for the ancient local custom where a two pence payment was made for every raven's head presented in the early efforts of pest control, the Victorian Black Swan Hotel, built of Lakeland stone in 1899, is home to a number of restless spirits. The village itself is rich in historic charm and enough local happenings to prove fertile ground for the raising of any number of wandering wraiths. A commemorative window in the Church of St Oswald celebrates Elizabeth Gaunt from nearby Brownber, who was 'the last female martyr burnt at Tyburn for the cause of the Protestant religion Oct.4, 1685'. To the north of the church, the now visible foundations of the Gilbertine Abbey built about AD 1200 were exposed by the excavations carried out in 1920, and St Oswald's also housed a 'Rights of Sanctuary' bell where any fleeing fugitive who tolled the bell once would be assured of a fair trial and possible pardon. The Black Swan itself has been noted as a hot spot for those attuned to psychic phenomena, the cellars of the hotel in particular occupied by 'Joseph', who walks the cellars in the company of

another spirit, that of an unnamed young woman who subsequently disappears underground. There is a possibility that the cellars of the Black Swan were at one time connected by a tunnel to a neighbouring building and that someone called 'Joseph' did in fact own and work in an adjacent business. Another unexpected apparition, possibly linked to a fire on site in 1897, has been known to manifest in the hotel's breakfast room, where the ghost of a lady in mourning garb watches over a coffin and is clearly not partaking of the hearty Cumbrian breakfast on offer.

An absorbing category of haunting, this chapter has provided only a taster of the numerous haunted public houses, inns and hotels throughout the Dales, and the author heartily endorses any further personal research on the part of the reader thirsting to make a more comprehensive investigation in the field of haunted hostelries in the Dales!

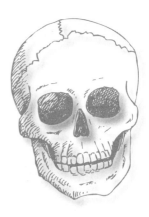

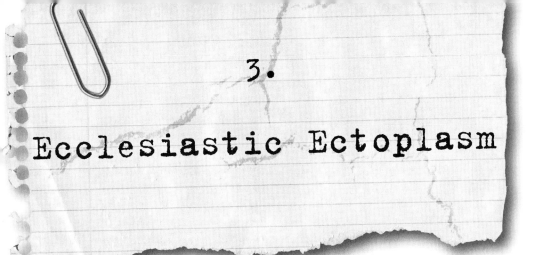

3.

Ecclesiastic Ectoplasm

WHILE one would usually expect those withdrawn from the secular world to haunt the site of their former religious houses, not all ghostly members of holy orders conform to this confinement. Locals of the Fox & Hounds in West Witton, Wensleydale would often offer advice to departing friends to 'watch out for the monk' on leaving the bar. The inn, built circa 1400, is Grade II listed and adjoins a separately owned building, the two together formerly known as 'Catteral Hall'. (The adjoining building, now a privately owned house, still bears this name.) Reputedly the oldest dwelling place in the village, the Fox & Hounds, was once a rest house for monks associated with

nearby Jervaulx Abbey – presumably this accounts for the still resident brother.

Further accounts of a hidden chamber within the inn's walls, just large enough to accommodate a single penitent sinner, may also date from this time, and the public house still retains an atmospheric rock-hewn cellar that some locals believe is connected by a secret tunnel to a one-time chantry chapel, concealed in the vaulted cellar of a fine house at the western end of the village. The house itself and the surrounding area of the village still bear the name 'Chantry', and sightings of a 'grey nun' in close proximity to the cellar exhibiting pre-reformation stonework also lend support to the supposition. However,

The Fox & Hounds, West Witton, abode of a ghostly monk. The famously good beer is stored in the atmospheric rock-strewn cellar.

another suggested course for this secret tunnel has been mooted, where a rather damp village footpath, aptly named Watery Lane, leads to a pile of stones known locally as the 'Giant's Grave' (the scary Giant of Penhill once terrorised West Witton).

Less than ten miles from West Witton are the picturesque ruins of Jervaulx Abbey itself, situated halfway between Masham and Middleham on the A6108. And perhaps the ethereal monk sighted by motorists on the sharp left-hand bend on the road approaching the abbey from the Middleham direction is making a hurried crossing back to the site of this former Cistercian house. The cause of many an emergency stop, startled drivers state that, on reaching a standstill, the figure of the monk simply disappears. Founded in 1156, the crumbling walls of Jervaulx (the name is Norman French and means Ure valley, a reference to the abbey's setting) now provide a beautiful backdrop for the flourishing habitat of wild flowers that now clothe the ruined stones, another vestige of the Dissolution of the Monasteries.

Another inn subject to holy orders as well as last orders is the Palmer Flatt Hotel at Aysgarth, another small village in Wensleydale and famous for its series of lovely waterfalls. As an aside, the church of St Andrew, which is located uphill from the tumbling waters, is reputed to have the largest churchyard in England, but none of the occupants of the many graves therein have a bearing on this public house haunting, as it is generated as a result of the hotel being built on the site of a mediaeval monastic hospice. Though the current building dates to the eighteenth century, the former hospice stood on the site during the Crusading era, providing care for pilgrims returning in ill health from the Holy Land. These pilgrims often carried palm branches with them as mementos of their journey, becoming known as 'palmers' and hence the hotel's unusual name. Allegedly run by the monks of the Order of the Knights Templar (a military order of fighting brothers founded in the twelfth century to better protect pilgrims travelling to Jerusalem, first introduced to Britain in 1146), the ghost of a white-robed monk who appears at the Palmer Flatt is accompanied by the smell of lavender, presumably to mask the scent of sickness and death. Less than three miles away, in a field at nearby Swinithwaite, the ruins of a Preceptory of the Knights

Jervaulx Abbey, home to the monk with a flagrant disregard for road safety?

The Palmer Flatt Hotel, Aysgarth.

Templar can be seen, where several stone graves still show through the turf.

On more traditional ground, so to speak, the solitary figure of a monk has been seen occasionally drifting around the riverside setting of the churchyard of St Michael's Church, Linton in Upper Wharfedale, perhaps waiting to cross the much photographed ancient course of stepping stones, once used by parishoners on their way to church, but impassible when the river is high. Though reports of this particular monk's sojourns are infrequent, who would be brave enough to refute the accounts of a royal witness, King George V? While staying at Bolton Abbey, the King verified the sighting of a ghostly monk seen by fellow house guest the Marquis of Hartington, which appeared outside his bedroom in the rectory in 1912. The Marquis described the ghost as a man in his late sixties with a heavily lined and wrinkled face, curiously round in shape, and had it not been for the several days' growth of grey stub-

ble on the ghostly chin may very well have been mistaken for a woman. A year prior to this sighting, the Revd MacNabb, rector of Bolton, was gazing out from one of the rectory windows when he felt a strong compulsion to turn around. On doing so he found himself being watched by an apparition in the doorway. Seen again in 1920 by Lord Cavendish and later in 1965 by a man entering the gatehouse who gave a clear description of an approaching figure dressed in a black cassock, white overlay, a black cloak and flat black hat, this same figure also busily frequented the ruined choir, the priory grounds and the vicinity of the church. The rectory was built on the site of the old priory infirmary using stones from the ruins, while the restored thirteenth-century nave of the abbey still serves as the parish church of St Mary and St Cuthbert today. No surprise then that that area of the priory should be such an active hot spot for black-robed spectres, as Bolton was home to the Black Canons, the Order of St Augustine. Seen by dozens of less illustrious witnesses, more recent sightings have been heralded by the strong smell of incense and favouring sunny days in July, with the apparition even drifting out of the priory grounds, onto nearby road and into houses. Further reports of an ecclesiastic figure seen trudging between the abbey and priory ruins describe the apparition as seemingly performing some unknown, unending task – perhaps as a form of spectral penance. Again, he is described as round-faced and unshaven, and whether or not he is the same apparition seen by the Marquis of Hartington, a deserving candidate for eternal atonement would be the corrupt Prior Moone, the last monastic superior of Bolton Abbey before the Dissolution, said to be bound to the abbey ruins. His favoured materialisation spot is beneath a particular carved roof boss which was described by John Walbran in his *Guide to Ripon* (published in 1837) as 'sagely conjectured by the country people to represent the devil'. Curiously, it has been posited that this Prior Moone and his less than exemplary antics are the origins for the nursery rhyme 'Hey Diddle Diddle, the Cat and the Fiddle', with the fiddle reference pertaining to the prior's less than scrupulous misappropriation of church funds – the cow jumping over the moon relating to his liaison with a local lady, and 'the little dog laughed to see such fun' linked with the two carved statues of dogs on the Bolton Priory tower, one of which appears to be laughing. There are four statues in total, one the depiction of a pilgrim with what appears to be a dish under one arm and perhaps the link to the last line of the rhyme 'and the dish ran away with the spoon', although it has been suggested that the prior's love object may have run off with the precious church plate!

Whether or not this is when the nursery rhyme first originated, the earliest printed version appearing in 1765, the rhyme was almost certainly in circulation long before the lyrics were first written down, and while many other hypotheses have been mooted, and we have no concrete evidence to support the Moone assumption, if true then it's no wonder that the prior's ghost should appear under the roof boss associated with the Devil himself.

Another dark association with the priory concerns the tomb of John, the ninth Lord Clifford and the supposed 'curse of the Cliffords', believed to be connected to a series of hauntings and disturbing occurrences experienced by a group of archaeologists excavating his tomb in 1973. Nicknamed 'the Butcher' or 'Black-faced Clifford', Lord John was at the forefront of the Lancastrian cause during the Wars of the Roses, and earned his black reputation when, after the resounding Lancastrian victory at the battle of Wakefield, rather than holding with common practice and ransoming the captured son of the Duke of York, Clifford was supposed to have killed young Edmund by his own hand, a murderous act verified by contemporary chroniclers and Shakespeare's vengeful portrayal of Clifford in *Henry VI,* Act Three. Whether or not this bloody Lord Clifford was responsible for the experience of something described as 'very black and evil' at the mouth of his freshly excavated tomb, the article appearing in the *Yorkshire Post* headed 'Curse Ends Tomb Search' summed up the archaeological team's catalogue of sightings of ghosts at the priory and even in their own homes. One of the excavation team even went so far as to refuse to continue with the exploration after falling ill while working on the tomb and blaming the Clifford Curse for his own poor health.

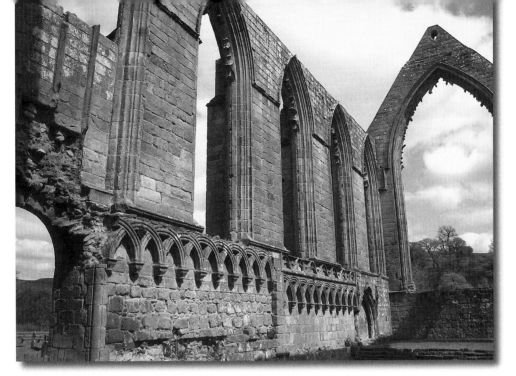

The ruins of the beautiful Bolton Priory, Wharfedale.

Clearly pharaohs don't have the monopoly on mortuary malediction.

However, at the lighter end of the spectral spectrum, Bolton's ruins are also said to be haunted by a white doe, the spirit of Lady Alice de Rumilly, owner of nearby Skipton Castle (later the seat of that cursed Lord Clifford) who gifted the land for the founding of the priory. More of this pious benefactress and her ungulate appearances hereabouts are covered in 'Phantom Four-legged and Feathered Friends'.

To date, no nursery rhymes have spawned from Fountains Abbey near Ripon, Britain's largest and some would say most dramatic monastic ruin, but reports of the hallowed harmonies of a disembodied male choir have been heard on several occasions, concentrated around the Chapel of the Nice Altars and usually heard at sunset. Founded in 1132 by the Benedictine Order, Fountains Abbey became one of the wealthiest in Britain thanks to the lucrative mediaeval wool trade, but the abbey's

The majestic ruins of Fountains Abbey.

wealth was to be its undoing as this lucrative house was one of the first to be subject to the brutal deconstruction brought about by the Dissolution of the Monasteries in 1540, so perhaps these haunting harmonies are the echo of pre-Dissolution evensong.

In addition to the haunting harmonies, another presence brought to public notice by an article published in the *Yorkshire Evening Post* in September 2008, in the form of a swirling smoke-like entity, was captured on camera at fountains, reinforcing stories of a ghostly monk in the vicinity of the abbey. Fountains also lays a tentative claim to being the one-time home to Friar Tuck of Robin Hood fame, the portly monk supposedly invited to join the Merry Men after challenging Robin to a sword fight. It is also said that Robin Hood's bow and arrows were once kept at the abbey – a rather figurative claim as a carving of the weapons can still be seen in the Lady Chapel, along with another nod towards the leafy connection in the fine carving of a 'green man' on the keystone of a window in the Chapel of the Nine Altars.

Somewhat more modest than the majestic Fountains, but still retaining echoes of its former monastic proportions, the picturesque ruins of the Easby Abbey, standing by the River Swale near Richmond, are most firmly associated with the local legend of the ghostly drummer boy said to inhabit a secret tunnel running between the abbey and Richmond Castle, the keep of which can be seen in the near distance (for more about this percussive phantom *see* 'Ghostly Sounds'). The abbey is said to be full of 'sonic ghosts', unusual as the monks were supposed to observe a strict rule of silence in the church and cloisters, with only necessary information conveyed by hand signals. While during the day only

the flapping of doves' wings is prevalent in the air, reports of ghostly noises and dark shapes moving around the ruins late at night lend weight to the tales of at least two 'white canons' still incumbent to Easby's environs. The brothers here were members of the Premonstratensian order founded in 1152 by Roald, Constable of Richmond Castle. Despite their code of austerity, in some instances the brothers strayed somewhat from the path. One was said to have committed suicide after the discovery of his affair with a local woman, and the other, a corrupt and greedy abbot of Easby, is presumably still restless having met an unrepentant end. In the same vicinity, the area between Holly Hill and the abbey is said to be occupied by the lonely figure of a nun patrolling the road hereabouts, and, obviously not entirely bound by her vow of chastity, she was supposedly walled up alive after an amorous liaison with a monk.

A happier sister frequents Ripley Castle, situated between Ripon and Harrogate, owned by the Ingilby family for over 700 years – believed to be one of the oldest families in the country to still occupy the same residence. The polite ghostly nun walks around the castle at night knocking on bedroom doors, but only entering when invited. Along with this considerate sister, the castle boasts a concealed priest's hiding place, and is also home to a host of other ghostly occupants – that of the 'Smoking Man' seen in the great hall flouting spectral health and safety regulations, along with the bedclothes-tugging phantom of a lady in late Victorian dress believed to be Lady Alicia Ingilby, whose two children died of meningitis here in the 1870s. Not an entire entity, the bottom half of another ghostly lady was seen to walk through two sets of closed doors in the vicinity of the Tower

Egglestone Abbey, former home to the Premonstratensian Order of White Canons.

Room by castle guides, itself an area which seems to be the focus of poltergeist activity. Located on the first floor of the Tudor Tower, alterations made in the 1930s led to the discovery of a fireplace behind the wood panelling, and in spite of the lack of external access and the room being locked and secured, the alterations seem to have provided a catalyst for the activity, as when workmen returned the next morning they found paintings in the furniture-strewn room turned to face the wall and the face removed from a grandfather clock – clearly the spirits guilty of these activities lacked the good manners of their fellow haunting sister.

More monks now, both seen along the banks of the River Tees; the first near the ruined Egglestone Abbey, which although possessing an ingenious toilet drainage system was nonetheless always a very poor abbey in comparison to the prosperity of other houses such as Fountains. Here along the riverbank, the figure of a searching monk, unusually brown-habited (Egglestone was a Premonstratensian house and the friars wore a white habit, so perhaps this figure in brown was a lay-brother) has been seen scouring the area for something obviously long-lost.

Just a mile and a half further downstream, where the Tees joins the River Greta at a place known as the 'Meeting of the Waters', another monk patrols the riverbank, having taken his own life in the river here. He shares this stretch of the riverside with the Maid of Rokeby (fuller mention of her unhappy floating apparition is made in Chapter 8).

An unlikely venue for a monastic manifestation, the impressive cave system at Ingleborough's famed Gaping Gill, one of Britain's longest and most complex cave systems and much loved by potholers, presented a curious experience to one caving explorer in the 1950s who noticed a glowing light behind him. On further investigation with his own lamp, the inquisitive caver was able to discern the form of a monk, who disappeared in front of him. In keeping with this theme of hallowed haunting, the capacity of Gaping Gill's underground chamber is said to be volume enough to hold York Minster.

Above ground and on former and firmer ecclesiastic turf, the ghost of a hooded monk, presumably of the Benedictine Order introduced by St Wilfrid, founder of Ripon Cathedral and responsible for building one of England's first stone churches here in the seventh century, has been spotted in the vicinity of St Anne's Almshouses on High St Agnesgate. The almshouses were built in 1869 in the gardens of the now ruined mediaeval 'Maison Dieu of St Anne', one of three such establishments which served Ripon for over 500 years, founded by one of the Nevill family in the reign of Edward IV. The ruined chancel of the chapel can still be seen in the gardens of the Victorian almshouses, carrying on the charitable tradition of the original St Anne's Hospital, endowed for the care of eight poor women of the parish.

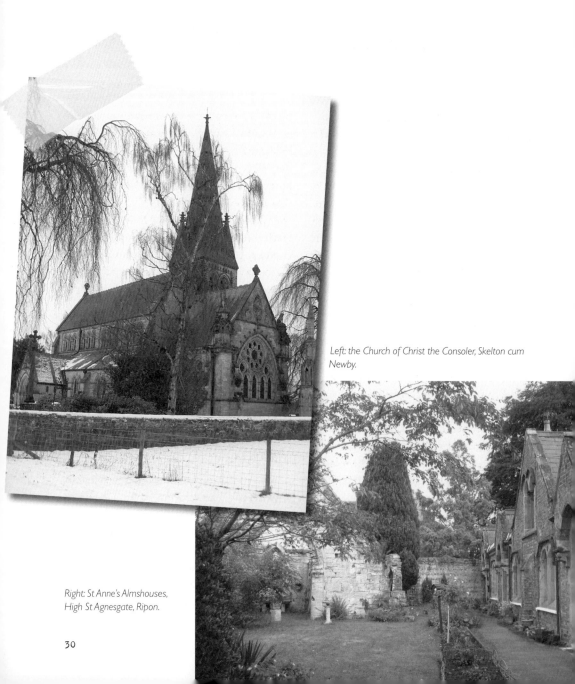

Left: the Church of Christ the Consoler, Skelton cum Newby.

Right: St Anne's Almshouses, High St Agnesgate, Ripon.

4.

Phantom Four-legged and Feathered Friends

GHOSTLY goings-on in the Dales are not confined to the human variety, as many examples of feathered and four-legged friends have been noted over the years, but probably the most frequently recounted animal sightings adopt the guise of the haunting black dog. While tales of spectral black dogs are legion throughout the British Isles, these creatures are certainly no stranger to the Dales, and while they are known by different names in different parts of the country – in Norfolk they are Shucks, Gallytorts in Suffolk, the Trash marauds in Lancashire, and Padfoots are seen in Staffordshire and the Wakefield area – our Yorkshire breed of dark hounds are commonly termed as Barghests. Numerously populating the district, the most famous of these is the 'Headless Hound of Ivelet Bridge'.

While Barghests can also take the form of other animals – pigs, goats and even donkeys have been noted – sightings do usually involve the entire animal, although the beast at Ivelet Bridge appears to be of the headless variety. One would assume that the sinisterness of this paranormal pooch would be seriously limited by its lack of head, thus rendering it unable to bark, let alone bite.

However, locally its appearance is regarded as a seriously bad omen, and as Ivelet Bridge is located on the 'Corpse Way', this belief may well have been encouraged in the past by the stories of burial parties seeing the dog run onto the bridge only to disappear over the edge, understandably lending more credence to the theme of ill fortune.

Many ghostly black dogs seem to have a preference for appearing on ancient tracks and lanes, which fits nicely with the Corpse Way, and their frequent proximity to water, either near ponds, bridges or fords could be explained as such crossings were often associated with the connection between this life and the next. Just wide enough for one car, the hump-backed Ivelet Bridge crosses the River Swale approximately a mile and half west of Gunnerside, and was described by historian Nikolaus Pevsner as the Dale's most romantic crossing (clearly he was unaware of the bridge's malevolent reputation). The 'Corpse Way' that crosses the single arched bridge (the name itself doesn't conjure up the jolliest of images), is a sixteen-mile path from the village of Keld along which the bodies of the deceased had to be carried for burial in the only consecrated ground in the upper dale at Grinton

– a very necessary journey bearing in mind that in mediaeval times if you weren't buried in consecrated ground then your soul was considered damned for all eternity. Along the route are a number of long flat flagstones where the wicker coffin would have been set down while the funeral party rested. On the north side of Ivelet bridge, set into the verge, is the Coffin Stone, one such place where weary pall bearers could rest their load on their journey from Muker down to the church at Grinton. This potentially hazardous two-day journey, especially in winter (there are records of pall bearers being swept away while trying to ford the flooded river at other points), incorporated a night stop-off at the Punchbowl Inn at Low Row, and here the corpse was stored in the imaginatively named 'Dead House' overnight. However, after the consecration of a Chapel of Ease and graveyard at Muker in 1580, the dead from the top of the Dale no longer had to make their final journey down the Corpse Way, which today is a popular route for walkers enjoying some spectacular scenery.

While black dogs do seem primarily connected with the death omen, their role as a harbinger of doom is not exclusive, as the 'Church Grim' demonstrates, a spirit that would appear to protect churchyards and the recently buried dead from the Devil, often materialising as a black dog and seen close to the church in stormy weather. Tales of black dogs providing a comforting, protective role have also been noted, there being occasions when a solitary woman on a lonely walk home would be accompanied by a Barghest acting as a protector, deterring any would-be assailant by the sight of such a menacing watchdog.

A 'protecting' black dog seen patrolling a lonely part of Wensleydale in the 1890s once accompanied a Wesleyan preacher on his homeward journey after making a charitable collection. Night had fallen and the preacher's route led him through a mile-wide wood. On finding a path through the dark, foreboding trees, he was surprised to be joined by a large but unthreatening black dog. Unable to make out where the animal had appeared from, he was aware that the hound remained with him, padding silently ahead of his horse. After safely emerging on the other side of the wood, the black dog disappeared with equal mystery. However, the story does not end here, and the preacher's relief at completing this hazardous section of his journey was dashed as he realised he had dropped his purse containing the precious collection money en route. Reluctantly turning his horse to retrace his steps, he was again joined by the black dog, which accompanied him back through the sinister wood, and on finding the purse stayed with the preacher again until he emerged safely from the trees. Many years later, two condemned prisoners in York jail recounted in their final confession how they had once intended robbing a Wesleyan preacher they had seen in those same woods on that very night, but were deterred from doing so when they saw the large black dog accompanying their would-be victim. Clearly a debt of gratitude was owed by the protected preacher, and perhaps paid by the retelling of this tale.

However, many dogs do bite, and another of the Barghest breed of a more malevolent nature is synonymous with Troller's Gill, the sinister limestone gorge near Appletreewick in Upper Wharfedale, also noted as the haunt of Scandinavian trolls, sprites and flesh-eating boggarts who like nothing better than to roll rocks down on those brave enough to enter the ravine. Almost 300 metres long, this popular walking route cuts deep into the limestone of Great Scar, ending close to Gill Heads where the remains of an abandoned lead mine can be found. In Parkinson's *Yorkshire Legends and Traditions* (1888) the huge and fearsome long-haired barghest haunting this ravine has eyes the size of saucers and razor-sharp saliva-flecked teeth. The tale of an intrepid local man (dating to 1881) intent on witnessing the beast for himself, recounts how he errantly set off one windy moonlit night, descending into the narrow and foreboding gorge, intending to spend the night. Despite taking the superstitious precaution of remaining within a circle drawn on the ground, reinforced with chanted protective charms and the thrice kissing of the damp ground on which he stood, on his challenging summoning of the barghest a howling wind blew up:

And a dreadful thing from the cliff did spring;
Its wild bark thrilled around;
And a fiendish glow flashed forth I trow,
From the eyes of the Spectre Hound.

Unfortunately, for our undaunted barghest spotter, the protective magic employed had no power to repel this particular Hell Hound and the body, later discovered by a shepherd, was said to exhibit wounds and marks not possibly made by the hand of man.

As well as the obvious potential for meeting a sticky end (assuming of course that you manage to avoid all the trolls and boggarts hurling rocks at you), an encounter with the Troller's Beast, which incidentally happens to be the size of a small bear, should on no account involve staring into his flaming yellow saucers-sized eyes, as to do so would result in calamity within a few days. This is a trait shared with the ghostly hound regarded as a harbinger of doom, supposedly

inhabiting the Sedbergh area on the northern fringes of the Dales.

An unusual variation on the demonic dog theme is the rainbow-eyed barguest seen about the village of Grassington, a few miles from Troller's Gill and noted as the 'capital of Upper Wharfedale'. However, the tally of visitors to one of the National Park's premier hot spots seems unaffected by this resident beast announcing itself with a rattling noise before materialising. There are even accounts of multiple dog sightings in the Dales, made by a cyclist returning from an evening church service in Swaledale back in the 1930s. Having reached Barton Quarry just after midnight he saw a 'dog-like figure', large with flashing eyes and foaming tongue, emerge onto the road. This first dog was grey in colour and was unexpectedly followed at 5-yd intervals by a succession of twenty further black specimens. Described as noiseless and resembling Old English sheepdogs, only much larger with shaggy coats and big heads, the cyclist saw a financial opportunity in selling one of the passing hounds at Darlington Market. However, after diving to capture one of the ethereal creatures, he ended up in a bed of nettles.

Still with the subject of canine manifestations, sightings of the wraiths of a man out walking his dog have been seen on the Stainforth Bridge, a packhorse bridge dating to 1675 built by Samuel Watson, local Quaker luminary and owner of nearby Knight Stainforth Hall. Spanning the Ribble before it plunges into Stainforth Foss, a dark pool 30ft deep in places, this spot is a favourite natural swimming pool in the height of summer. The picturesque and incredibly narrow stone bridge was given over to the protection of the National Trust in 1931, and has been the chosen haunting spot for this one man and his dog since the ghostly tennancy of their one-time home was curtailed when part of Knights Stainforth Hall was destroyed by fire some 200 years ago. The bridge formed part of their walking route between the Hall and Dog Hill. The idyllic setting of Stainforth Bridge encourages many visitors to the area, with the additional entertainment value of traffic attempting to negotiate the sharp angle onto the bridge and its continuing sinuousness; hair-raising enough without the added obstacle of ghostly pedestrians.

Turning to those dogs of a more mysterious nature, the vanishing variety has been seen in the environs of Richmond Castle, the now impressive ruin of one of the greatest Norman fortresses in Britain. Perched on a rocky outcrop overlooking the River Swale, it was originally built to subdue the unruly North of England. Now in the care of English Heritage, both staff and visitors have reported mysterious dogs spotted inside locked buildings within the castle precincts, who have then disappeared.

Another vanishing hound, later signifying an omen of death, was seen on the A684 near Leeming Bar, bordering the eastern edge of the National Park, by two women on their way to Northallerton in the summer of 2001 between 8 p.m. and 10 p.m. The driver, making an emergency stop, shut her eyes in anticipation of the deadening thud of a dog running from the kerb into the path of her car. However, her passenger gazed on in amazement as she saw the large black dog pass through the bonnet of the braking vehicle; the shadow-like hound had floppy ears but no distinct facial features. As a final gruesome twist to their experience, a man who the women recounted their tale to later committed suicide, reinforcing the superstition that the appearance of black dogs signifies an omen of ill fortune.

However, such foreboding signs are not solely restricted to canines; tales of a phantom black cat are rife in the village of Thwaite. The community is famous for being the birthplace of pioneering nature photographers Richard and Cherry Kearton, and also the likely location of Misselthwaite Manor in Frances Hodgson Burnett's *The Secret Garden*. Whether this large black moggy ever came close to being captured by the Keartons' camera, or indeed prowled about Mary Lennox's prospective hidden flower beds, the fateful feline was renowned for its habit of sitting on the doorsteps of those cottages whose occupants were deemed not long for this world, an unwelcome sight that perpetuated in the village for over a century.

An entire pack of spectral hunting hounds can be heard baying in the area around Mill Beck in Harmby – where locals have long avoided walking after dark, as here the murdered Lady of Hernebi (an old name for Harmby) takes the shape of a phantom white doe. One Jordayne de Hercla supposedly killed the unfortunate lady, but revenge came her way one day when de Hercla was out hunting and spotted the highly prized trophy of a white doe. Of course, unbeknown to him, he was in fact stalking Lady Harmby in her wraith form. However, before he could deliver the death blow to his captured quarry, de Hercla collapsed and died on the spot which was said to be over Lady Harmby's grave; divine retribution indeed, as the spirit of de Hercla and his hunting pack is said to forever wander Mill Beck, stalking the unattainable phantom white doe.

Another ghostly white doe frequents the ruins of Bolton Abbey, said to be the spirit of Lady Alice de Romilly. The priory was originally founded around

1120, on land gifted to the Augustinian canons by Lady Alice, owner of nearby Skipton Castle – possibly her attempt to secure a heavenly place in the next life, or as an expression of her grief at the death of her only son, known traditionally as 'the Boy of Egremont'. Young Romilly had tragically drowned in the Strid (more of the tempestuous and dangerous stretch of the River Wharfe later) while exercising his greyhound, the dog refusing to make the jump and causing his master to fall and drown. However, the latter supposition for Lady Alice's gift is unlikely as the boy's name later appears on the deed granting Augustinian monks further land to relocate the priory, as the original site near Embsay was in an exposed position. Nevertheless, Wordsworth's poem 'The Founding of Bolton Priory' recounts the loss of the Boy of Egremont to the violent waters thus:

And hither is young Romilly come,
And what may now forbid
That he, perhaps for the hundredth time,
Shall bound across 'The Strid'?

He sprang in glee – for what cared he
That the river was strong, and the rocks were steep!
But the greyhound in the leash hung back,
And checked him in his leap.

The boy is in the arms of Wharf,
And strangled by a merciless force;
For never more was young Romilly seen
Till he rose a lifeless corse.

Bolton Abbey's associations with white does and Wordsworth do not end here. Another legend connected to the priory tells that after the Dissolution of the Monasteries and the establishment's subsequent demise, a white doe would appear in the abbey churchyard every Sunday and remain throughout divine service, only to disappear when the congregation emerged. The creature was said to return to Rylstone Hall, home of the ill-fated Norton Family and basis for another of Wordsworth's poems 'The White Doe of Rylstone'. After a visit to the the priory ruins in 1807, Wordsworth was inspired to write the poem, using the cemetery adjoining the eastern and northern sides of the priory as the setting for his narrative verse based on the local legend of melancholy Emily Norton. After the downfall of her family, who were participants in the doomed 'Rising of the North' in the reign of Queen Elizabeth I, Emily finds herself consoled by a white doe, befriended in her childhood and now her only friend left in the world. Even accompanying Emily on her visits to her brother's grave, the sad tale concludes with the creature faithfully continuing Emily's graveside vigil after her own death: 'Why thus the milk-white Doe is found, Couchant beside that lonely mound'.

From white does to white geese, the church gates of St James the Great in Melsonby form the backdrop for a phantom fowl's vanishing act. The tale involves a farmer who was driving his pony and trap back from market in nearby Richmond when his horse suddenly shied and bolted. Struggling to regain control and still travelling at some speed, the farmer was amazed to see what appeared to be a large white goose waddling along at matching velocity beside the out-of-control trap, only to vanish through the locked churchyard gates at the end of the track. Over time the ghostly goose was seen by several people on a number of other occasions, and even eluded the clutches of two local poach-ers who, returning home one night with a lighter-than-normal bag, failed to swell their ill-gotten gains when their quarry vanished into thin air as they made a grab for it.

Often mistaken for flocks of wild geese, Gabriel's Ratchets is the term applied to the supernatural pack of flying spectral hounds heard and sometimes seen in the skies over North Yorkshire. These monstrous aerial dogs, also called 'sky yelpers' and some-times described as possessing human heads, were a sure portent of ill fortune and death. Believed by some to be the ghosts of unbap-tized babies hovering around the parental home, and seen by some as spectral birds with glowing eyes appearing to those with a relative or friend near death, the appear-ance of these harbingers of misfortune were described by David Naitby, schoolmaster at Bedale, in his diary entries for October 1773. After three instances of the Ratchet Pack appearing in the skies over the town, on 18 October he wrote: 'But seven nights now gone since Gabriels raced overhead, and now there has come to us a blood red moon, a sure sign we are to be judged for our sins.' It seems that whatever form the Ratchets assumed they were surely a terri-fying omen in years gone by.

Another bizarre avian apparition was reported by three people exploring the cave systems around Chaple le Dale, renowned potholing country and home to the famed 'Hurtle Pot' (for more about this murky water-filled pool *see* 'Ghostly Sounds'). Described as dark blue and much larger than a bat, the creature glided slowly past them, and defies any reasonable explanation.

A treasure-protecting phantom black hen inhabits the environs of the ruined Pendragon Castle, near the hamlet of Outhgill in remote Mallerstang Dale.

Reputedly built by Uther Pendragon, sup-posed father of the legendary King Arthur and a fifth-century chieftain who led local resistance against the invading Anglo-Saxons. According to tradition, Uther and 100 of his men were killed at Pendragon Castle when the Saxon invaders infiltrated the water supply by poisoning the castle well. It is also claimed that the Romans constructed a temporary fort here, as the road connected their forts at Brough and Bainbridge. However, despite the lack of architectural evidence supporting either of the stages of earlier construction, (the ruins of the existing Norman castle date to the twelfth century) the legends of Uther's ghost still hold, as do the tales of the hoard of treasure hidden here but protected by the phantom black hen that avidly replaces any soil dug up by the treasure-hunters. The current ruin, standing on private land but open to the public, was most probably built by Hugh de Morville, who incidentally is also said to haunt the site as punishment for his part in Thomas Becket's murder.

The strong tradition of hidden treas-ure being safeguarded by hens, cockerels, ravens and eagles (some even consuming the odd foolhardy treasure hunter) links in with the account of another guardian rooster relayed in *Notes on the Folk-lore of the Northern Counties of England and the Borders* by William Henderson (1879) and pertain-ing to a hoard of buried gold in Swaledale, possibly hidden by retreating Celtic tribes-men who were renowned for their fine gold jewellery. Henderson wrote that he had learnt the following:

...from Mr. Robinson, of Hill House, Reeth, Yorkshire, that in his neighbour-hood as in many others is a place called Maiden's Castle, in which tradition avers a chest of gold is buried. 'Many attempts,' he

The atmospheric remains of Pendragon Castle, near Outhgill.

says, 'have been made to gain possession of the treasure, and one party of adventurers actually came up to the chest and laid hold of it, when a hen appeared, flapped her wings, and put out the light'. This occurred three times, and the men were obliged to desist. The next day was Sunday, but still they returned to the place. A violent storm of thunder and rain came on, however, and the 'drift', in miners' phrase, 'ran'. My informant, an old man of the place, knew this, he said, for a fact.

Yet another hen is involved with the legend of the giant's treasure concealed beneath Stony Raise Cairn, the round barrow to the south of Addleborough Hill near Bainbridge in Wensleydale, and the obstacle which caused the giant to lose his grip and drop his precious load. It is said that to this day the treasure remains beneath the cairn and that bizarrely it can only be uncovered with the assistance of a hen and an ape! Why an ape should be involved is unexplained, but needless to say this theory has yet to be put to the test.

In the market town of Leyburn (one of the principal market towns on the east side of the Yorkshire Dales which has developed as the traditional centre for mid-Wensleydale and gateway to the Dales National Park) in an unassuming residential semi, streams of phantom livestock regularly traverse the living room for upward of two hours at a time. Located near to the old town pound – a stone structure used for keeping livestock, often holding straying animals until a fine could be levied on their owners – the footprint of this property clearly lies en route to market place, as the frequency of these ethereal herds of cattle and sheep re-enacting the journey to market would suggest.

By the 1680s, the population of Leyburn (around 300 souls) was large enough to warrant a market, the first a Michaelmas market held on 29 September 1684 under a charter granted by Charles II. Held in the present market square, originally on alternate Tuesdays, by 1686 the market had increased and was held every Friday. Today, with an increasing area given over to the parking requirements, Leyburn town square is far too busy with the bustle of people and traffic to make a livestock market feasible. Consequently, sales have now moved to the

Leyburn Auction Mart on the Richmond Road, where auctions are still usually held each Friday, and on a point of interest is still en route for the sitting room stampede.

Finally we move on to the Strid, a notorious stretch of water where the River Wharfe is forced through a deep, narrow gorge holding a dark reputation, as where the channel diminishes to its slenderest point of mere two metres wide, the foolhardy are often tempted to jump. The width of the gap looks a deceptively easy leap but the varying heights of the rock ledges on either side – which are often very slippery – have given rise to the saying that nobody ever fails the jump twice, as one false step invariably proves fatal, as demonstrated by the death of the 'Boy of Egremont'. Maintaining a safe distance is advisable as the powerful currents running through this turbulent channel will suck down any unfortunate into the underwater caves and eroded chambers that lie hidden beneath the churning surface, which perhaps gives rise to the descriptions of our final and only equine ghost, that of the pale horse said to rise from the foam of the Strid every May Day. While accounts vary, the phantom palfrey is usually accompanied by a fairy who promises to grant human wishes and reveal details of the seeker's future. But these promises belie a malevolent reputation, as both horse and fairy's annual intent is to drown anyone foolish enough to come too close to the rapids. This fate befell three sisters from Beamsley who, many years ago, thought they'd try their luck one May Day morning, only for their bodies to later be recovered washed further downstream. Known as the Airedale Poet and writing until his death in 1843, John Nicholson's 'Lines on the young lady who drowned in the Strid' allude to a further tragedy in the watery demise of 'young Eliza', and while these cautionary tales may be the mere invention of those wishing to reinforce the dangers presented by the fierce running waters of the Strid, this wild and beautiful place still holds the potential, either through earthly bravado or a spectral harmful hand, to spoil anyone's bank holiday.

The tempestuous Strid.

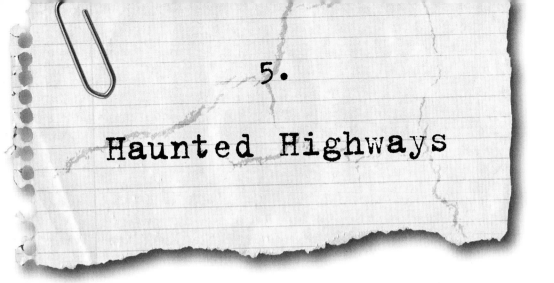

5.

Haunted Highways

Ghosts on the Open Road

From headless highwaymen to phantom coaches, haunting hitchhikers and tragic traffic dodgers, the roads, lanes and paths of the Yorkshire Dales provide plentiful accounts for the haunted highways in the district.

What better than a horse-drawn carriage to capture the modern romantic imagination? But perhaps not so enchanting when one realises that such sightings are commonly regarded as a portent of death. In many instances both horses and coachman are headless; however, all the components of our first phantom coach and four appear intact, in this recurring haunting around the roads of Aysgarth in Wensleydale. Though the spectacle has been noted in various other locations in the upper valley, the route and destination remain a mystery. With more specific locations in mind, a team of four spectral horses pulling a phantom coach apparently passes by Brunton House in North Craven. Though the house is now situated rather off the beaten track on a minor drovers' road, on a slight deviation of the A65 between the top of Buck Haw Brow and the hamlet of Feizor, in July 1753 the Keighley to Kendal Turnpike Trust decided to route the turnpike along Brunton Road, placing Brunton House on one of the main routes from York to Lancaster. Given the location, it is safe to assume that Brunton House was at one time an inn. However, the origins of this haunting must pre-date 1792, as by this time it had been decided that the gradient at Rawlinshaw Brow was too steep for horse-drawn coaches, and the route was changed from the top of Buck Haw Brow to pass below the scar of Cave Hole and down to the line of the present A65 – once again Brunton House was isolated from the main drag, unless of course the phantom coachman's map-reading skills are akin to those of the author.

A few miles from Brunton House, the old turnpike route along Buck Haw Brow takes the traveller to Settle, a bustling market town with a wealth of interesting shops, welcoming cafés and historic buildings. Home of the famous Settle to Carlisle Railway, the area is also associated with a different, more spectral, form of transport in the shape of another phantom coach. Driven by Sir Henry (son of the fourth Earl of Northumberland who, despite being a Yorkist supporter during the Wars of the Roses, refused to fight for Richard III) the frantic coach flight is the reenactment of the Earl and his family escaping the vengeful Yorkist rebels. This horse-drawn drama was last seen on 3 September 1885, but any further anniversary appearances have failed to materialise. Another ghost coach with an aristocratic spectral occupant is a well-known manifestation on Skipton's High Street. The appearance of Lady Anne Clifford in her horse-drawn coach at midnight, heading for the gates of Skipton Castle is said to herald the death of the current lord of the castle. The only surviving child of George Clifford, the third Earl of Cumberland, Anne was born at Skipton in 1590 but her age and sex presented obstacles to her inheriting the estate on the death of her father in 1605. The determined Anne (renowned by her contemporaries for an unyielding personality) finally won the long and complex legal battle to obtain the rights to her inheritance in 1643, and perhaps her struggles in this respect account for the fact that her appearances precede the impending transference of her one-time hard-won estates.

Our final coach and four audibly haunts what was once the back drive of a former grand house in Chapel House Woods, Kilnsey, again favouring midnight as the witching hour. Other noted nocturnal activities in the fields surrounding Kilnsey concern a circle of dancing fairies, who, in gratitude for a passer-by refraining from disturbing their dance, rewarded him with the gift of a ring of mushrooms the following morning. One would hope that the rumble of carriage wheels has never interrupted the merriment of the little folk hereabouts.

Still dealing with equine emanations on the Dales highways, we turn to highwaymen, both with and without heads. Our first candidate is the famously flamboyant gentleman highwayman John 'Swift Nick' Nevison. Operating during the

seventeenth century, Nevison was alleged never to have used violence against his victims, somewhat romanticising highway robbery. His reputation was further heightened by his renowned overnight ride from London to York, often erroneously attributed to Dick Turpin. Nevison supposedly once evaded capture after performing his famous horseback leap off Giggleswick Scar, this place still marked on ordnance survey maps as 'Nevison's Nick'. There are two explanations as to how Nevison's horse was able to make this mighty leap – the first is that after allowing his horse to drink from St Alkelda's Well, situated at the foot of Giggleswick Scar beside the road which runs from Settle to Clapham, the healing holy waters from this renowned 'Ebbing and Flowing Well' revived his mount sufficiently to perform the feat. The other theory is that the female spirit inhabiting the well gave Nevison a magic bridle that gave his horse legendary abilities. The water in the well does in fact periodically ebb and flow, sometimes brimming over onto the road and other times being at least 8 ft below the edge of the stone trough into which the well water runs. Though no conclusive cause for the water's actions can be established, there is a legend that, in an attempt to evade the amorous pursuit of a lusty satyr, a water nymph's prayers were answered when she escaped the satyr's clutches after the gods turned her into the well; the tidal ebbs and flows of the water are supposedly caused by her eternal breath. A charming story; unfortunately St Alkelda's Well no longer sinks and rises with breathy regularity since the rhythm of this phenomenon was interrupted by the misguided excavation of the well many years ago. Despite replacing all of the stones exactly as they had been found, today the well has been reduced to a rather more erratic performance; but it is still a marvel nonetheless, and perhaps an endorsement to the old adage 'if it ain't broke, don't fix it'.

Another celebrated highwayman, though not as gentlemanly as Swift Nick Nevison, Tom Hoggett is said to patrol the course of the old Great North Road between Boroughbridge and Scotch Corner, waiting to pounce on the unwary as he did in life. A swift-moving apparition with a long coat dragging along the ground, he lights his way with a bulls-eye lantern. Tom drowned in the River Swale while trying to escape the law, trading the inevitable hangman's noose for a lung full of water.

Operating on another of the main trade routes between Kettlewell and Kirkby Malzeard, crossing through Coverdale and over the aptly named Dead Man's Hill (more of this haunted location later), another thieving Tom was Tom Taylor, renowned for his cruelty and indiscriminate highway robbery, often killing unfortunate travellers in cold blood before making off with his ill-gotten gains. Starting out as part of a gang specialising in robbing isolated farmsteads, Tom branched out on his own to pursue a more lucrative career in highway robbery, with his secret lair in the now infamous cave in How Stean Gorge known as Tom Taylor's Tunnel. Accessing his hideaway by scaling the rocks at the side of the gorge or scrambling through a hidden entrance concealed by tree roots, Tom's secret cave is now a popular feature of How Stean Gorge. This remarkable surface limestone formation first became a tourist attraction in the Victorian era with a gala opening on 18 August 1869, admission one shilling to

Tom Taylor's cave hideout, How Stean Gorge, Nidderdale.

include a brass band performance. Today's visitors to the gorge are offered the option of a torch on entrance for a minimal charge – which is a must if one is to fully appreciate the amazing cavern where Tom Taylor would hide and count his money. We must assume that the locals who finally caught up with Tom and hanged him from the metal bar still apparent in the roof of the beehive chamber were equally well illuminated. The rough justice meted out by them gave rise to the tales of Tom Taylor's ghost still haunting the cave.

Travelling the same trade route favoured by Tom Taylor, the headless, restless, vengeful wraiths of three murdered Scottish pedlars are said to haunt the aptly named Dead Man's Hill, the high ground separating Coverdale from Nidderdale, where in 1728 their decapitated corpses were found buried in the peat, the theft of their money and goods the obvious motive. Travelling the packhorse road running from Middlesmoor in Nidderdale and over the

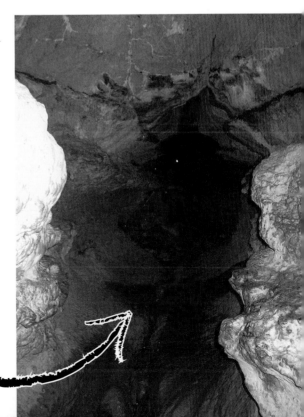

summit of Dead Man's Hill to Arkleside, the unfortunate trio were supposedly murdered at a wayside inn in the now ruined hamlet of Lodge, overlooking Scarhouses Reservoir. However, the finger of suspicion was firmly pointed in the direction of the proprietor of one of the two other local inns in the village of Horsehouse at the time, located on the Coverdale side of Dead Man's Hill, and the village so named as the packhorse trail merged hereabouts with one of the main coaching roads between London and the North, making Horsehouse an important staging post for travellers and drovers alike seeking rest and a change of horses.

Not surprisingly, the naming of Dead Man's Hill has encouraged a number of tales concerning where and by whose hand the three pedlars really did meet their end. There has even been some suggestion that the pair of stone outcrops on the moor above Ramsgill, some five miles to the north-east of Dead Man's Hill and known as Jenny Twigg and her daughter Tib, may be connected with the murders. Albert Winstanley, veteran cyclist and travel writer of over half a century, included in his book *The Golden*

Wheels of Albert Winstanley (1985) a section entitled 'Over the Hill of the Dead Men' where he recounts the same tale of the unfortunate headless Scots, but this time, claiming they fell victim to a murderous landlady and her daughter accomplice who ran an inn in Arkleside, the tiny hamlet at the top of the hill today comprising of a sprinkling of farms and houses. The inn at Arkleside has long been converted to a private dwelling, but Winstanley proposed the link between the wicked mother and daughter rock combo, who in legend were turned to stone as punishment for their misdoings. Millennia of harsh elements have shaped these pillars of millstone grit into forms resembling contorted human faces. Another account tells of an evil inn keeper running a drovers' inn located on the summit of Dead Man's Hill, where the unwary were systematically murdered in their beds – robbery being the motive, although the only hint to the existence of such a notorious establishment today is a pile of stones on the top of the hill, the site of so much alleged wrongdoing having long since been pulled down.

Another highway robbery is commemorated on a stretch of the A684 at Akebar,

Dead Man's Hill, seen from the Nidderdale approach across Scar House Reservoir.

along the section known as Conyers Lane between Constable Burton and Partick Brompton. Here a memorial stone at the side of the carriageway known as 'Nichol's Stone' is inscribed with the now badly weathered words 'May 19, 1826 Do No Murder'. This sandstone ashlar slab reputedly commemorates a local cattle dealer murdered on the spot by a farmer who spotted him driving some livestock to Leyburn market back on that May day in 1826. Lying in wait and waylaying the dealer on his return journey for the pocket full of money his cattle had made at sale, the murderer was subsequently brought to justice and hanged at York, his body buried in unconsecrated ground outside the churchyard of nearby Finghall church where he is said to have sought sanctuary for a while. Known locally as the 'Murder Stone', during the carriageway widening works carried out on this stretch of A road some twenty years ago, it was found necessary to relocate the stone to a position further back on the verge. However, superstition runs strong in these parts and it was some time before the foreman could find enough men willing to touch the Murder Stone, let alone move it. To this day, those passing Nichol's Stone on particularly dark, moonless nights who are aware of the evil deed it commemorates, report feeling an eerie foreboding about the spot and a distinct compulsion to put the pedal to the metal.

Located on the road between Grassington and Skipton, the village of Rylstone (probably best known for the Rylstone Women's Institute nude charity calendar – the inspiration for the film *Calendar Girls*) also lays claim to a haunting highwayman, although details of his manifestation are sketchy and his wraith has made no appearance since before the First World War. More, however, is known

The Nichol's Stone or 'Murder Stone'.

of the headless horseman seen at Linton, less than four miles from Rylstone on the Grassington road, a village noted for its sloping green with central flowing beck spanned by several bridges – namely a clapper bridge, a packhorse bridge, a road bridge as well as ford and stepping stones, and ranking Linton as one of the prettiest villages in the Dales. The rider, dating to the time of the Civil War was a Royalist messenger carrying a vital document from Skipton to be delivered to Royalist sympathisers in Linton. Waylaid en route by a Parliamentary patrol near Cracoe the Royalist rider was decapitated in the subsequent skirmish, but somehow, despite his lack of head, the messenger continued on his journey, desperate to fulfil his mission, and dropped from the saddle, along with the letter, at the feet of Linton's local curate. You may surmise, however,

Tessie Parla.

that as this ghostly ride was re-enacted over and over in an attempt each time to deliver the precious paper into the right hands, possibly the curate may have been a Cromwellian man who disposed of the message according to his sympathies. But as the sightings have ceased in recent years, perhaps this headless messenger is now content to rest, having finally delivered his document into the rightful (presumably ghostly) hands.

Still in the age of horse and rider, the Revd Nicholls' *The History and Traditions of Ravenstonedale* holds an account of a mounted phantom and steed, said to have accompanied one Richard Bousfield, an adamant disbeliever in the existence of ghosts, one dark night when he was riding back from Blasterfield to Ravenstonedale village. While passing through the Sunbiggin area, he was joined by a silent man on horseback who mysteriously appeared at his side 'whom he could not pre-cede, or follow, or leave in any way until he came within sight of the village'. One would presume this experience may have altered Mr Bousfield's outlook as to ghosts and their possible existence.

Tales of another phantom mounted on a spectral steed are firmly rooted along another stretch of the A684, this time around the sharp bend in the road between West Witton and Swinithwaite in Wensleydale, by an outcrop of rock at the roadside known locally as 'Tessie Parla'. The site of many a vehicular 'prang', the surprise appearance of the horseman is frequently employed as a convenient excuse far outweighing the usual causes familiar to most motor insurers.

Another odd occurrence on this section of road concerns an old man who, returning home on foot to Swinithwaite, was surprised to be greeted by his dog with wagging tail in the middle of the road. On affectionately greeting his hound, the animal simply disappeared. Somewhat perturbed, he nevertheless continued on his journey and, once home, recounted the story to his wife, who insisted that the dog had been with her all evening. While in this instance there were no grounds to suppose that the sighting was alcoholically induced, another incident where a local man was forced over a dry stone wall in

West Witton by the rearing apparition of a horse and rider was preceded by an evening of warm hospitality in the Fox & Hounds. I leave the reader to draw their own conclusions.

This same stretch of road leading out of the village of West Witton has also been associated with sightings of 'earth lights' – haunting floating lights, familiar to ancient peoples and regarded as fairies by the Celts, though the Welsh knew them as 'corpse candles' and believed them to be harbingers of death. The West Witton light appears as a dazzling, glowing ball emitting an extremely high-pitched noise not unlike a dog whistle, but vanishing on the approach of vehicles. A similar flickering light defying explanation has been disconcerting motorists in the vicinity of East Scrafton in neighbouring Coverdale for many years. Known as the 'Pennine Light', this intense beam seen floating down the middle of the road and often mistaken for an approaching motorcyclist has been associated with the nearby St Simon's Well, a spring of water formerly used as a healing bath. The ruins of an oratory chapel dedicated to the saint close to the well is traditionally held as the resting place of St Simon the Cananaean and apostle, and whether or not these holy remains are the catalyst for generating the unearthly glow, perhaps this is the same dazzling globe seen in West Witton, possibly migrating across from the neighbouring dale around closing time.

Still with highways but this time on foot, a phantom hiker has been seen on the footpath linking Caldbergh (neighbouring village to East Scrafton) to St Simon's Bridge. Though last seen nearly fifty years ago, described as bearded and wearing an old-fashioned hacking jacket and leather leggings, he asks for directions in a Scandinavian accent before simply vanishing.

The lanes and footpaths around the village of Appletreewick, a picturesque little village in the heart of Wharfedale, echo to the sounds of a set of phantom footsteps. The footfalls are said to be those of a wraith wracked by guilt after surreptitiously moving his neighbours' boundary markers in order to gain more land for himself. Eventually his conscience got the better of him and he took his own life. Remorseful over his actions, and also for the outstanding payment owed to the pharmacist who'd sold him the poison used to end his life, this penitent phantom was finally laid to rest after an encounter with a local man (fortified by spirits of another kind) who agreed to replace the boundary markers and pay off the chemist bill. After this was done, his guilt assuaged, the remorseful spirit was never seen again. Another ghost walker of a friendly nature has been encountered on the network of footpaths above Appletreewick, variously appearing as an elderly farmer or a teenage hiker and usually joining visitors to the area on their walk; however, he doesn't offer much in the way of conversation as he vanishes as suddenly as he appears.

At nearby Burnsall, the riverside village in Lower Wharfedale situated by an ancient packhorse bridge crossing a bend in the River Wharfe, another more grisly pavement pounder takes the form of a lonely walker sighted on winter's evenings. Not firmly identified but possibly the ghost of one Thomas Denholme, dressed in the garb of an early Victorian gentleman farmer, he presents a shocking apparition with his skeletal face and empty eye sockets. His emaciated body was found in his home several months after his death in 1842, but his debut appearance was not recorded until the 1980s and, if this ghostly identification is cor-

Burnsall village, haunt of the empty eyed lone pedestrian.

rect, the reason for his delayed haunting is unknown.

A more melancholy and sightless pedestrian manifestation patrols the A685 between Kirkby Stephen and Ravenstonedale. 'Bad' or 'Blind' Lord Wharton earned both sobriquets, supposedly struck blind in divine retribution for the evil treatment of his tenants as Lord of the Manor and President of the Peculiar Court of Ravenstonedale. Struck blind one night while riding home, this well-dressed but mud-spattered lord has been seen at the roadside walking erratically, trying to find his footing. In spite of the pitiable sight, his withered hands covering his sightless eyes, no passer-by has ever offered assistance as it is said that the first kindly word or gesture will break his eternal torment.

Finally, we turn to the restless souls of those involved in tragic road traffic accidents. Our first example of this relatively recent form of haunting was actually the cause of further accidents rather than the victim of one. At Wigglesworth on the fringe of the Dales, a stone's throw from the A65 between Settle and Skipton, on the road to Tosside, the recurring spectre of a fleeting female form dashing in front of traffic has resulted in a number of car accidents along this stretch of road. Her form picked out in car headlights, locals hold that the apparition is generated as a result of the death many years ago of a young serving girl who had been sent to fetch water from a nearby stream but who fell in and drowned.

At Ingleton, on a road leading out to Lancaster, the victim of a road traffic accident was knocked down and killed in 1937. However, for several weeks after the death, motorists reported repeat sightings of a 'blue man' stood in the road at the site of the accident. The unfortunate motorists stated that having failed to swerve to avoid him, the blue man would simply vanish on ethereal impact with their vehicle.

The ghost of a schoolboy supposedly knocked down and killed by a cart many years ago has been seen crossing the road outside the hospital chapel of St Mary Magdalen in Ripon. Favouring dusk in the early weeks of winter, the unfortunate lad has also been seen within the precincts of the chapel itself, founded in the twelfth century to care for lepers and blind priests, and now presumably forlorn schoolboys.

On the road to Rathmell near Settle, close to the packhorse bridge crossing the Rathmell Beck, is the spot where the grieving ghost of a First World War soldier's widow appears in the middle of the road, the location where the unfortunate woman was knocked down by a straw- laden wagon. Clearly distracted, on her way to break the sad news to her mother that her husband had been lost in action (he was reported missing just two days before the armistice), the distraught widow failed to notice the approaching wagon. She did in fact survive the accident

The road outside St Mary Magdalen.

but sadly lost her baby a few weeks later. Understandably, when the poor woman caught a chill her will to live was tenuous at best and, succumbing to pneumonia, she died. However, a few weeks after her death her ghost made its first appeared near the packhorse bridge, in the middle of the road facing on-coming traffic, clad in the long grey coat she had been wearing when she set out on her sad journey and will continue to wear until her spirit is laid to rest.

Then Came the Railways

It would seem apt to include within Haunted Highways those of the railed variety carrying the iron horse through the Dales. The most celebrated railway falling into this remit is surely the epitome of Victorian railway engineering – the Settle to Carlisle Railway. Trains journeying along the 72-mile line through the Dales pass over the twenty-four-arched Ribblehead viaduct – built between 1870 and 1875, a most impressive sight standing some 30m tall and running approximately 400m across the valley floor – before clat-

tering on through the longest tunnel on the line at Blea Moor. The trains emerge in Dentdale and on to Garsdale before leaving the Dales through the Eden Valley and arriving at the border city of Carlisle. The many navvies employed by the company to build the railway lived rough on the surrounding moors, and hundreds lost their lives in the construction of the line with pick and shovel, many being buried in the churchyard of St Leonard's at Chapel-le-Dale. They are commemorated by a Dent fossilised-marble plaque, which was put up in memory of the men from the 6,000 strong workforce who died and whose ghosts are still said to restlessly inhabit the bleaker moors through which the railway cuts.

Blea Moor tunnel itself is reputed to be haunted by some of those unfortunates killed during its construction – with reports of uneasy rail passengers overcome by a cloying, sickly sweet smell filling the carriage – they are being somewhat relived to see the light at the end of the tunnel. The Blea Moor signal box also carries its own paranormal reputation based on the story of a signalman receiving a heavy breathing call from a lineside phone in the middle of the night – long after the track gang's shift had ended and over half an hour after the last freight train had passed through.

On the Selside section of the line, a large male figure known as 'Big John' has been seen on the track by signalmen, only to suddenly vanish as mysteriously as he appeared – perhaps one of those unfortunates who failed to see the completion of the line in 1876 after seven years of hard toil. The line is further tinged with tragedy as on Christmas Eve 1910 the incident known as the 'Hawes Junction' rail crash claimed twelve lives. The crash was caused when a busy signalman forgot that a pair of light engines were waiting on the northbound side of the line bound for Carlisle, and on clearing the signal for the approaching high-speed Scotch Express travelling from St Pancras to Glasgow, the express and light engines collided just after the Moorcock Tunnel near Ais Gill summit, almost entirely derailing the express train with disastrous consequences. Casualty numbers were exacerbated as the timber-bodied coaches over-rode each other and then fire broke out, fed by the leaking gas feed for the coaches' lighting and ignited by the coals from the steam locomotives' fireboxes. The bodies of the unfortunate twelve victims (some were trapped in the wreckage and horrifically burned to death) were stored in the cellar of the nearby Moorcock Inn, which served as a temporary mortuary before subsequent burial in the churchyard at Hawes. The Moorcock Inn itself (the present building dating back to the 1740s) is reputedly occupied by some meddlesome furniture-moving manifestation, but it is unclear whether these happenings stem from the use of the pub cellar as temporary mortuary or another tragic incident in 1975 when a fire claimed the lives of the then owners. If it was a malevolent spirit who had a ghostly hand in this more recent disaster, it has made its presence felt anew to the current owners. Coinciding with the arrival of a fire safety engineer who came to service the inn's fire extinguishers, a framed newspaper article detailing the more recent tragedy in the inn's history inexplicably fell from the wall and smashed to pieces. Was this possibly a spectral protest on the part of this potential pyromaniac presence, aggravated by the maintenance of fire fighting equipment designed to thwart any further designs? On further consideration, it is more likely that any heat generated on the premises today would be confined to the warm and welcoming atmosphere radiated by the Moorcock's wood-burning fire.

The Moorcock Inn.

6.

Ghostly Sounds

Things That Go Bump in the Night

What can be more haunting than an auditory phenomenon? The unseen utterance, things that go bump in the night? What about ghostly melody? Muffled strains of sixteenth-century music have been heard at Middleham Castle, the now extensive roofless ruin that was once the fortified royal palace and childhood home to Richard III. Built to guard the district of Coverdale and protect the road from Richmond to Skipton, many of the stones from the now defunct imposing bastion found their way into the fabric of some of the houses in the town, now famed as a centre for race-horse training. Sounds of battle have also been heard in the vicinity of the castle accompanied by a ghostly charging knight on horseback thundering down from the direction of the first motte and bailey structure at Middleham called William's Hill, the mound of which sits some 250 yds behind the current castle. More intriguing still are the rumours of a hoard of buried treasure somewhere in the grounds. It is said that if you run around the castle three times, where you stop the treasure will be found; sadly, though, nobody thought to record a starting point for this race to riches and so the treasure and the tale remain intact.

Perhaps the percussive force of falling water lends a favourable ambiance to hearing supernatural speech, as at Hardraw Force waterfall, where the angry raised voices of three former friends have been heard, usually during a thunderstorm, as it was in such weather that one of the men was killed. The body,

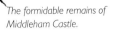
The formidable remains of Middleham Castle.

when found, was retrieved at the foot of the falls, claimed to be England's highest single-drop waterfall with a reputed 100ft descent to the plunge pool below. It was initially thought to be a suicide. In actuality, marks of apparent combat covered the man, but in a further twist, these injuries were obscured by what turned out to be a post-mortem plummet. Even more spookily, later, evidence was found at the top of the falls in the form of a fused and melted dagger. Could it be that the cause of the man's death was divine retribution in the form of a lightening bolt from the heavens striking down the unworthy party in the argument? The body of this non-conductive individual remained buried a the nearby cross-road in accordance with custom and the law that suicides and convicted criminals be denied burial in consecrated ground – the crude form of the cross presented by such a bisection of highways being the next best thing. (Crossroad burials were officially abolished by Act of Parliament in 1823.) Incidentally,

Hardraw Force waterfall is set within the grounds of the historic Green Dragon Inn, and access is unusually gained through the bar of this thirteenth-century traditional country public house where liquid outpourings of another kind can be enjoyed. In addition to the angry men, the Green Dragon itself boasts a plethora of pub spirits; the spirit of a playful young boy has been sensed – it would appear that he mischievously likes to roll small balls of light across the parlour bar floor. Also known to frequent the public house are a mead-making monk (spotted in the former scullery), a former owner from the 1960s who, when not seen, can be heard sitting on the creaking fireside chair, a wraith-like servant girl, and a safety-conscious entity who has been known to move boxes of firelighters around.

Various reports of inexplicable noises of a watery working nature also abound at the former Watermill Inn (the licence was transferred to the adjacent Bridge Inn in 2003) just outside Pately Bridge, where at the turn of the nineteenth century this water-driven flax mill was powered by the still operational 36ft diameter water wheel, famed as one of the largest overshot wheels in England. After the mill's closure nearly forty years ago, strange creaking and groaning noises were reported in the vicinity, but no satisfactory explanation was ever found for the sounds of mysterious milling activity.

Another former water mill, Yore Mill located on

The former Watermill Inn, near Pately Bridge.

Yore Mill, Aysgarth Falls.

the River Ure at Aysgarth Falls, is pictur-esquely set against one of Wensleydales's most famous beauty spots, with the waters tumbling over a series of broad lime-stone steps forming the upper, middle and lower falls; a favourite feature for visitors making a bee-line to the Aysgarth Falls National Park Centre. Built in 1784 by Birkbecks of Settle, the four-storey Grade II listed former cotton mill is one of the earliest examples of an 'industr-ialised' mill outside of an urban setting. Now housing a café and a number of visi-tor attractions of the arts and crafts variety, the mill was once home to the Yorkshire Carriage Museum (now sadly closed) which claimed a phantom in one of the then exhibits, a haunted cab. Another ghost is said to audibly frequent the building, the son of one of the former mill owners who, as a result of the attempted seductions of a number of female mill hands found him-self minus some 'vital parts' after a spot of rough justice was meted out, supposedly accounting for the high-pitched screams heard from this sorry lothario.

Kirkby Stephen, in the former old county of Westmorland, is a traditional market town remote from larger populations. The Monday livestock market still held in the market square, dating back to the town's original charter granted in 1352, is still an important event in the town and surround-ing countryside. Kirkby Stephen boasts many historic buildings and structures, and Frank's Bridge, the seventeenth-century corpse lane bridge supposedly named for one Francis Birbeck, a local brewer, still retains coffin stones where the dead could be rested on their way from the nearby hamlets of Hartley and Winton. The bridge is said to be haunted by the auricular ghost 'Jangling Annas'. Making her pres-ence known with the jangling sound of her chained wrists, Annas was an escaped prisoner from nearby Hartley Castle, the thirteenth-century home of Sir Andrew de Harcla (now only a fragment of the mediaeval castle wall remains in a farm-yard). Jangling or 'Jingling' Annas, as she is otherwise known, drowned in the river beneath Frank's Bridge, probably inhibited

Frank's Bridge, Kirkby Stephen, said to be haunted by 'Jangling Annas'.

from the breaststroke as her hands were supposed to have been reduced to stumps by the manacles she was forced to wear during her confinement. Today, however, Annas may have to increase the volume of her jingle jangles in order to be heard over the noisy population of macaws flying freely around the town, their loud squawking and occasional chatter a surprising and colourful feature of daily life in Kirkby Stephen when these beautiful parrots are not at home in their private aviary on the outskirts of town.

Not all ghostly sounds are of a lamentable nature, as at the Goat Gap Inn, Clapham; in one of the rooms the sound of children reciting nursery rhymes has been heard. Set back from the A65 between Ingleton and Settle, on what used to be the old drovers' road, this whitewashed former farmhouse with an unusual goat-shaped weather vane is a popular traditional inn. An exorcism carried out some years ago provided a temporary abatement in the nursery

recitations but the children aren't the only spectral inhabitants of the Goat Gap as 'George' (the nickname given to the ghost of a former farmer) enjoys nothing better than to watch the goings-on of the temporal world from one of the front windows of the public house. He is in good company with 'Sally', another resident spook, not to be confused however with 'Sally' the inn's resident goat! Childish sounds of a more plaintive nature have been heard at Fairthwaite Park House near Kirkby Lonsdale, where a murderous former owner of the house in the late eighteenth century was thought to be responsible for the disappearance of a number of children in the local area. While the suppositions of distraught parents remain unproved, on cold winter nights it is said that the sorrowful cries of young voices can be heard, and indeed terrified a visiting party of Girl Guides back in the 1960s.

The resonance of more sad children comes from beneath the surface of

Thruscross Reservoir, one of the quartet of Washburn Valley's reservoirs (Fewston, Swinsty and Lindley Wood are the others) and beneath which lie the submerged but not always hidden remains of the village of West End. Evacuated at the beginning of the 1960s to enable construction work to begin on the dam creating the highest of the four reservoirs, the remains of demolished dwellings and the stumps of felled trees have re-emerged on occasion from the surface of Thruscross during periods of dramatic low water levels, namely the summers of 1989 and 1990 and during the drought of 1995. In amongst the remaining visible rubble are the stones of a workhouse once located at the centre of the village, where it is said that children were kept in the harshest of conditions along with the adult inmates and that, on still evenings, their pitiful cries can still be heard.

More spooky speech has been heard in the ghostly vocalisations emanating from Swinsty Hall, the beautiful seventeenth-century manor house on the south-eastern edge of Fewston Reservoir. Could the phantom 'hellos' be the greeting of the Hall's builder, a man called Robinson who was said to have died a lonely man after being shunned by friends and neighbours. Though this sounds uncharitable, those unwilling to associate with Robinson had an understandable motive as they feared contagion after his return from plague-stricken London where he had spent a profitable interlude robbing the dead and looting abandoned houses. Often seen washing his gold and silver in the Greenwell Spring, these ill-gotten gains equipped him financially to build the Hall, but he could never wash away the taint of wrong-doing and died sad and alone.

From mere 'hellos' to full-on outcries, reports of chilling screams come from Barden Tower, the ruined former fortified hunting lodge on the edge of the road leading up Lower Wharfedale between Bolton Abbey and Burnsall. Before the tower fell into a ruinous state after the lead and timbers were robbed from the building in the 1780s, a high-pitched echoing scream was often heard from within the walls and, while these cries terrified visitors, the locals simply tolerated the unearthly sounds with unflinching acceptance as a 'shout from hell'.

The area around Barden itself has been described as the 'Barden Triangle', an expanse of supposed supernatural activity encompassing the villages of Appletreewick,

Barden Tower.

53

Burnsall, Linton and Grassington, each village in turn claiming varying haunting manifestations of their own. Also within the boundaries of the triangle is the haunted limestone gorge of Troller's Gill (further details of this malevolent location are covered in 'Phantom Four-legged and Feathered Friends') as well as Elbolton Hill – 'Hill of the Fairies' – one of the strangely shaped Cracoe Reef Knolls inhabited by the little folk and said to possess magical properties. Also falling within this mysterious wedge of Lower Wharfedale is Dibble's Bridge, supposedly built by the Devil, in a moment of rare generosity assisting a local shoemaker who shared a drink with him. Nearby Dibb Gill is associated with the exorcism of another noisy ghost, Thomas Preston, owner of Low Hall in the seventeenth century. He terrorised the inhabitants of Appletreewick and Lower Wharfedale with his bangs, groans and yells. The spur for his hauntings, dating to the mid-eighteenth century, are unknown but the disturbances were percussive enough to unseat ornaments. A priest finally laid the spirit in the gill, hence the area is now known as Preston's Well.

Still with chilling vocalisations, further high-pitched screams emanating from a ghostly floating skull have been heard in the area of Gibbet Hill in Grass Wood, now a nature reserve to the north-east of Grassington. One plausible explanation could be the gibbeting of a convicted murderer's corpse in these woods, one Tom Lee, an inhabitant of Grassington who, though twice released after being charged with the murder of the local physician Dr Petty in 1779, was finally convicted at York and subsequently hanged. His body was suspended and left to rot as a gruesome and brutal reminder of the fate of those convicted in the era when capital punishment was still prevalent.

Further audible visitations from the executed, in the form of hoots of heinous laughter, have been heard in the area around Middleton and Barbon, once the haunt of the infamous Smorthwaite Gang. These seventeenth-century hooligans indulged in robbery, sheep stealing and coin clipping amongst other crimes for which brothers Henry and William Smorthwaite were finally hanged in 1684. (Little hope of clemency with the draconian 'Hanging' Judge Jeffreys presiding.) Late-night occupants of cars parked in the vicinity are initially alerted to the brothers' phantom reclamation of their 'patch' by grinding and rasping noises, followed by grisly laughter culminating in visions of grotesque faces being pressed against car windows – a real passion killer!

More ghostly sounds in the form of heavy phantom footsteps have been heard along the riverside walk at Linton. This footpath leading from the village to Linton Falls, a beautiful cascade formed by the River Wharfe as it rushes through a series of limestone bedrock channels, has clearly always been a popular path, as over the years the collective sound of many walkers has been heard, but the sound of the feet always dissipated on investigation. However, we are on more solid ground so to speak with the ghostly footsteps of one of Ripon's former Wakeman, the city official originally charged with the task of warning Ripon's populace of any impending peril by sounding the 'Wakeman's Horn'. Traditionally blown at 9 p.m. every evening to 'set the night watch' at the four corners of the obelisk in the Market Square, and coinciding with the curfew sung in the nearby minster tower of Ripon Cathedral, this is an unbroken tradition of over 1,000 years standing. The office of Wakeman became that of Mayor in 1604, and it is in the Mayor's house, built in the sixteenth century and a rare surviving example of early timber-framed construction, that the white-clad ghost of Hugh Ripley, the city's most famous Wakeman and first Lord Mayor, has been seen at the upper windows. Generations of the Precious family, who occupied the Mayor's house for nearly a century from the 1820s, were often woken by Hugh's footsteps, who wasn't averse to a spot of furniture movement either, when not busy making an appearance in one of the front bedroom windows.

It Came From Below...

Ghostly sounds are not only confined to above ground, as bumps, scrapes and even the sound of clogs have been noted from various underground locations around the Dales. But let us begin with the legend of the lost congregation at Kirkby Lonsdale where, if you put your ear to a large dent in the ground on the area of Cockpit Hill, it is said that you will hear the singing of a church full of people who were swallowed into the earth on this very spot. Cockpit Hill forms part of the remains of a small motte and bailey castle that today, perhaps aptly, is part of the nineteenth-century extension to the nearby St Mary's churchyard. Another thread of Kirkby Lonsdale folklore has the Devil throwing a large boulder at another local church, creating a depression now known as the Devil's Punch Bowl, a geographical feature in Underley Park to the north of the town, beneath which the church is said still to be buried – deep underground but still intact.

A well-famed and noisy child ghost is incorporated into the many legends associated with Richmond Castle, the impressive ruin of one of the Conqueror's defences perched in a commanding position above the River Swale. The famous and widely known story of the 'Drummer Boy' tells of an unfortunate lad lowered into the mouth of a newly discovered passageway which the soldiers garrisoned at Richmond believed linked the castle to nearby Easby Abbey. He was told to beat his drum so that the subterranean route could be marked out by the

The Mayor's house, Ripon. A rare surviving example of an early timber-framed dwelling, constructed around the sixteenth century, today the Wakeman's House Café.

listening soldiers following his progress above ground, but midway the sound of drumming ceased and the little drummer boy never emerged. Even after several centuries, it is said that his drum beats can be heard as he makes his way along the mysterious lost tunnel. On the footpath between castle and abbey is the 'Drummer Boy's Stone', a monument with a plaque reading:

> According to legend, this stone marks the spot where the Richmond drummer boy reached in the tunnel supposed to lead from Richmond Market Place to Easby Abbey. Here the sound of his drumming ceased and he was never seen again.

Richmond Castle also lays claim to the famous Arthurian legend of Peter Thompson, a local potter who found his way in (or was shown by a mysterious stranger) to a cavern below the castle via a tunnel – perhaps the same one the drummer boy still inhabits – where King Arthur and his knights slept, ready to be awakened in time of national need. Thompson came upon Arthur's sword and horn lying on the ground next to the slumbering warriors. Though frightened, curiosity drove the potter to partially draw the blade, but on so doing the knights began to wake – terrified, he replaced the sword and understandably forewent blowing the horn, instead running for the entrance. As he fled, a voice boomed 'Potter Thompson, Potter Thompson, if thoust had drawn the sword or blown the horn, thou hadst been the luckiest man e'er born'. Thompson supposedly blocked the entrance hole and it remains hidden to this day.

From booming voices to rhythmic throbbing, a curious noise can be heard after heavy rain, pulsing up from the subterranean depths of the 'Hurtle Pot', the

Richmond Castle, perched imposingly over the River Swale

The mysterious 'throbbing' Hurtle Pot.

opening to a water-filled cave near to the Church of St Leonard in Chapel-le-Dale. This noise, along with the blame for anyone who unfortunately drowned in the pool's deep waters, was attributed to the resident ghost said to live in the Pot. However, the rush of water through the system after heavy surface rainfall is a more likely and earthly explanation for the pounding noise. In 1983, cave divers were called in to perform an unusual rescue when they retrieved a statue from the 30ft of water then filling the Pot. The sculpture, an interpretation of an archer by Charles l'Anson (though rather unkindly described by some as resembling an alien) had been thrown into the water by vandals. However, the statue has now been reinstated in its original location on

the lane to Whernside Hill, and is now additionally thought to be protected by the presence of the Hurtle Pot.

Moving on in a mining vein, the extraction of lead ore has been a traditional industry throughout the Dales for thousands of years, especially in the Nidderdale area. The Nidderdale Museum, housed in the former workhouse in Pately Bridge, features displays depicting the important quarrying and mining history of the area, complete with a reconstructed mine tunnel. And it goes without saying that, employed in such a dangerous industry, the many spirits of those lost to the commonplace hazards of collapse and flooding are said to still frequent the levels. Not surprisingly then, deep within the Greenhow lead mines ghostly miners have been heard working and moving wagons around long after the shift of the living had ended, while the noise of metal scraping on metal has kept awake those above ground for the best part of the night. At nearby Stump Cross Cavern, now acknowledged as one of the most impressive show caves in the country, ghostly footsteps have been heard. Discovered by accident in 1858 by two mining brothers prospecting for lodes, the cave's poor yield seemed commercially unviable, but the enterprising William and Mark Newbold saw the potential of opening the caverns to the public with an admission cost of one shilling. Though entry costs a little more than a shilling today, the superb stalactites, stalagmites and other curiously shaped mineral structures within the limestone cave system are well worth a visit. And perhaps the same ghostly feet from Stump Cross fill the invisible echoing clogs mysteriously heard on the roads around the village of Greenhow Hill, the small former lead-mining settlement close by.

Further evidence of former mining activity also litters the landscapes around Swaledale (care should always be exercised as unmarked concealed openings arising from disused mine works can present a hazard to the walkers), and one such shaft near the village of Keld is the basis for the curious tale of Charles Mannion, a retired Richmond schoolmaster who decided to go exploring one sunny afternoon in 1924. After a pleasant lunch and armed with a lamp, sensible Charles set off to investigate through the overgrown entrance he'd found to an old mine shaft. Clearing away the undergrowth, no sooner had he entered the mine than he was stopped dead in his tracks by what he described as a human voice warning him, by name, to withdraw. Initially thinking this a trick of the wind, on hearing the warning and his name repeated several times Charles ran for the safety of the entrance, reaching the opening just as the roof collapsed behind him. Could this perhaps have been the cautionary voice of one less fortunate, the spirit of a miner still trapped within? Possibly another curious mine enthusiast, though less fortunate than Charles Mannion, the skeleton of 'Buckden Bill' was discovered in 1960 in Buckden Gavel Mine on the western flank of Buckden Pike, where the moor is still heavily scarred with shake holes (pronounced 'shackles') and the spoils of the lead mining industry. Entering the mine some time in the 1890s, perhaps this unfortunate gent was a former miner come to reminisce about his working life, or a curious villager come to investigate the ghost stories of the 'Old Man', the ghost of a lead miner said to frequent Buckden Gavel from long before. Whatever the reason, his body was discovered in 1964, some 400 yds from the mine

entrance, and when the Upper Wharfedale Fell Rescue Association later made a fuller investigation of the workings, it was noted that clog marks could still be seen in the mud on the floor, made by the last men to work at Buckden Gavel more than eighty years previously. While the personal effects found with the skeleton threw no light on the identity of 'Bill', the sixpenny piece dated 1872, two shilling pieces dated 1885 and a funeral card for a presumed friend or family member (one John Winskill who had been buried at Settle in 1890) served to establish a rough date of death, even if the hows and whos remain a mystery. As an aside, at least the safety requirements for visitors to one of the Dale's subterranean features today consist of more than a walking stick and a felt hat, which is all 'Buckden Bill' was equipped with.

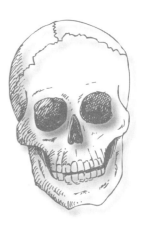

7.

Military Manifestations and Spectral Soldiers

The Romans

The Roman occupation of the Dales lasted for over three centuries (from approximately AD 79 to 410) and therefore allowed plenty of time to pack in some ghostly reminders of their military presence, along with the physical evidence of their enforced grasp on this part of the Empire's northernmost provinces, still seen in the remains of military camps and telltale Roman roads throughout the district. Some forts, such as the one at Catterick (to this day retaining a garrison) developed into towns, and the visible domestic remains of villas at Piercebridge and Aldborough testify to this. Along with the archaeological evidence, vestiges of the Roman presence can still be felt through lingering legionaries making the odd ghostly appearance.

Situated on the Roman road running through Stainmore and leading on to Cataractonium, or Catterick as we now know it, the ruined remains of the keep of Bowes Castle were constructed on the foundations of the Roman fort Lavatrae. Built in the late first century, traces of the fort are still visible in the fields south of St Giles Church; the fort protected

the Roman road on its course across the north Pennines, the modern route now followed by the busy A66. During the final days of the waning occupation and a general disintegration in discipline, the garrison stationed at Lavatrae went on a plundering spree of the surrounding villages, laying their hands on anything of value, especially gold. Eventually, the victimised locals banded together in enough numbers to storm the fort in a revenge effort and massacred the Roman soldiers within. However, clearly suspecting a local backlash, the soldiers had already secretly buried all the ill-gotten loot. But, with the entire garrison annihilated, the hidden location remains unknown to this day. It is said, though, that on the anniversary of the massacre, the ghosts of the murdered soldiers appear at Bowes Castle to re-enact the burying of the treasure. Associated folklore dating to the sixteenth century tells of two local men who had the splendid idea of hiding in the ruins on the anniversary, so that they might observe the ghostly legionaries and ascertain exactly where to dig. They claimed to have seen a procession of soldiers carrying a huge chest of gold which they then watched them bury. However, before the location could be disclosed, both men met a violent death within hours of each other. The first was murdered by his greedy associate, who, on proceeding to scrabble in the dirt at the appropriate spot, was beckoned by a mysterious blood-red hand and dragged over the fields to the banks of the River Greta, where his body was discovered the next day. Understandably, for many years Lavatrae was shunned as a dark and sinister place, especially around the anniversary of the bloodbath that had taken place so many centuries before.

More lost legionaries are said to still wander the imaginatively named Pockstones Moor, an area of desolate and sparsely populated moorlands to the south- west of Pately Bridge, boasting the striking grit crags of Great and Little Pockstones. Destined to eternally drift lost about the moor, these unfortunate soldiers were possibly a massacred troop sent to eliminate the remains of one of the rebellious Brigante tribes who sought safe haven on the moors after the final defeat

of their leader Venutius at Stanwick in AD 71. Venutius was the husband of the more widely known Cartimandua, queen of the Brigantes and 'client ruler' for the Romans. However, Cartimandua tired of her union with Venutius (she remarried his armour bearer Vellocatus) and, in seeking to overthrow his ex-wife, Venutius unsuccessfully took on the might of her Roman protectors who ultimately crushed the tribal uprising. While the ghostly Roman soldiers, heard arguing on their trudge in the direction of Barden Fell (perhaps a disagreement over direction) may well have fallen victim to the vengeful Brigantes, it is equally possible that on this open moorland they simply died of exposure. Another physical reminder attributed to Venutius's resistance to the Romans can be seen in the landscape in the form of a ditch known as 'Tor Dyke', forming a defensive trench close to Great Whernside and cut by the valley road that steeply descends on its approach to Kettlewell. The man-made linear fortification, linking in with the natural escarpment, stretches for

The site of Lavatrae, now beneath the remains of Bowes Castle.

The Hunter's Stone on lonely North Moor, Coverdale.

some three miles and doubtless would have seen many engagements and skirmishes between native Brigantes and invading Romans. There are several ancient yet artificial mounds scattered about this part of North Moor, suggesting the burial sites of the fallen Celtic tribesmen from nearly 1,000 years ago and giving rise to local legends of the restless spirits of slain warriors still haunting their old battleground.

Just half a mile from Tor Dyke, on the lonely road crossing North Moor heading for Horsehouse, is the Hunter's Stone. Set by the roadside in the shadow of Great Whernside, usually the first recipient of the early winter's snows, this nearly 7ft guidestone made from sandstone marks the now remote but once important route – used by monks and drovers – connecting Kettlewell with Coverham Abbey. Incised with a small cross on one face, now incredibly worn with the ravages of time and the elements, the Hunter's Stone is said to perform an unusual party piece in that when the clock at nearby Hunter's

Hall (now re-named Coverhead Farm) strikes midnight, the Hunter's Stone spins around. North Moor is a truly breathtakingly desolate landscape, and a popular stopping point for those wishing to take advantage of the footpaths criss-crossing the moor up Whernside and dropping down into Kettlewell. However, I have yet to come across anyone willing to visit this lonely spot for any length of time after dark in the company of the buried fallen Brigantes, let alone wait until midnight to see if the Hunter's Stone really does twirl.

On the south-eastern fringe of the Dales, near the Roman town of Aldborough, a lone centurion called Flasius who died while defending the garrison is said to still patrol a stretch of the busy A1, the course of which largely follows Dere Street (the Roman road running north from York and crossing the River Ure here at Aldborough). Isurium Brigantum, to give the town its Roman name, may have been the base of the famous Ninth Legion who, under the command of Caesius Nasica, had put down the revolt led by Venutius. One can only assume that the earlier death of Flasius excluded him from the later fate of the Ninth, who were massacred by Queen Boudica, and he has remained fixed to this spot to continue guarding the marching route taken by his legionary colleagues.

The Dark Ages

Moving forward along the timeline of armed apparitions, a ghostly army of upwards of 100 raggedly dressed warriors has been sighted around Blea Moor, now one of the classic locations traversed by the Settle to Carlisle Railway as it descends off the Whernside fells heading for Dentdale. Thought to be Viking raiders who troubled these parts in the Dark Ages, they obviously thought enough of the area to settle rather than merely ravage the surrounding countryside, as the remains of a viking farmstead show (excavated at nearby Ribbleshead, and vestiges of the Norsemen's occupation still exist in many of the placenames hereabouts). Between Whernside and Gragareth lies the wide glaciated valley of Kingsdale, still sometimes known as the 'Valley of the Vikings' and home to Yorda's cave. This former Victorian show cave, comprising a large main chamber and underground waterfall, was, according to Norse mythology, the former home of the Norse giant Yorda, but presumably he'd moved out before Charlotte Brontë's visit to the cave as it is thought to have been the inspiration for the 'Fairy Cave' in her novel *Jane Eyre*. However, another identity has been mooted for these phantom soldiers streaming from the hills – that they are the ghostly remnants of a band of Scots

'moss troopers' – bandits who were either disbanded or deserted from one of the Scottish armies during the period of the English Commonwealth, who retained their weapons and subsisted by plundering from civilians and Parliamentary soldiers alike. A difficult differentiation to make as, in life, both the Norse and Scots marauders caused widespread terror throughout the area.

A more firmly identified Viking, Eric Bloodaxe, the fearsome red-headed ruler of the kingdom of Northumbria, is said to haunt the sight of his last engagement, with his final battle-cry carried on the howling Pennine wind. In AD 954, Eric met a sticky end along with his son Haeric and his brother Ragnald at Stainmore. Betrayed by Earl Oswulf, who had treacherously led Eric to believe he could rely on his martial support, the spot where Bloodaxe fell is marked by an ancient stone cross, the Rey Cross, located just to the south of the A66, five miles west of Bowes. Now moved to a lay-by position post carriageway works, the Rey Cross (now complete with information board) was once the marker denoting the boundary between the Dark Age kingdoms on either side of the Pennines, with Viking Danes in the east and Norwegian Vikings in the west. However, the demise of Bloodaxe ended the Viking domination of the Jorvik kingdom, and the might of the Norsemen was not to be felt again until the accession of King Cnut.

From Dark Age cries carried on the wind to ghostly militia marching through the lower troposphere, in 1881, on several occasions throughout the year, phalanxes of phantom soldiers were seen marching through the skies above Ripley village. Described as one of North Yorkshire's treasures with its stone cottages and cob-

The Rey Cross. The author was saddened to find the purported resting place of Eric Bloodaxe now set into a rubbish-strewn lay-by on the busy A66 spattered with vomit.

bled squares, the deserved reputation of the village itself is somewhat overshadowed by the historic Ripley Castle, set among the deer park, lakes and walled gardens created by 'Capability' Brown and ancestral home of the Ingilbys. As to the brigade of sky-bound troops, a former owner of Ripley Castle may provide a link to the unusual apparition as, in 1644, Sir William Ingilby, supporter of the Royalist cause, fled the battlefield for his ancestral home when the Parliamentary army prevailed at Marston Moor. The site of the Battle of Marston Moor itself has long been associated with sightings of ghostly Cavalier soldiers, and at Ripley the exterior east wall of the fifteenth-century ancient parish church of All Saints still bears evidence of bullet holes, believed to have been made by a Parliamentary firing squad executing Royalist prisoners who were taken after their crushing defeat. Sir William, however, fared somewhat better, as on reaching Ripley Castle (with Oliver Cromwell hotfoot in pursuit) he was

hidden in a priest hole within the castle by his sister Jane. This gutsy sibling, on reluctantly allowing Cromwell to enter the castle, held the future Lord Protector at pistol point all night, thus preventing a search of the house. Jane's determination won the day and, deterred by this display of feminine bravery, Cromwell departed the following morning empty-handed. For her part in the drama Jane was henceforth known as 'Trooper Ingilby'.

More Recent Martial Manifestations

From sky-borne spirit soldiers to those who patrolled the skies during the Second World War, we have a number of tales linked to allied airmen and aircraft. The first comes from RAF Leeming, which became operational as a bomber station in July 1940, mainly operating Whitley, Stirling, Halifax and Lancaster aircraft. Stories of a Second World War bomber crew in wartime flying kit spotted walking together have been linked to the area on the base once used as the bomb store at the remote southern end of the air field. In the vicinity of a mound of earth concealing the wreckage of a crashed aircraft, even when not actually visible, the phantom airmen have been heard laughing and joking with one another.

One would hope that the RAF officer and flight crew whose briefing session was detected by psychic investigators visiting the historic Kiplin Hall fared better on their missions. Built in the 1620s for George Calvert, first Lord Baltimore and founder of Maryland, USA, Kiplin Hall at Scorton near Richmond is host to a number of active spirits (twenty-five at the last count!) and in particular those associated with the Hall's requisition by the RAF in the Second World War. Most commonly reported are the the numerous strange presences and 'smellings' in the old kitchen, converted into a flat for the use of RAF personnel, with the strong aroma of pipe and cigar smoke frequently detected on the air – presumably an olfactory hangover associated with the wartime operations that took place at the hall.

The sad tale of another 'downed' allied aircraft is associated with Hag Dyke near Kettlewell. A Wellington bomber from a Polish squadron crashed on the snow covered hillside of Buckden Pike, claiming the lives of all but one of the crew. The surviving airman crawled down to Hag Dyke, now a Scout hostel administered by the first Ben Rhydding Scout Group in Ilkley, but at the time a farmhouse. Following fox tracks in the snow, believing this would lead to habitation (knowing a fox's proclivity for obtaining domestic fowl), the airman is said to have subsequently died in a bedroom at Hag Dyke, now the drying room (not 'dying room' as some have joked) for

the hostel. However, there is an alternative and brighter end to this story as the injured airman, Joseph Fusniak, the plane's rear gunner, did manage to drag himself and his badly broken ankle along a trail of snowy fox paw prints, which led him to the village of Cray where he was spotted by the daughter of the landlord of the White Lion. Despite initial suspicions that he was a German pilot in view of his limited English, he made a full recovery. But Hag Dyke is still reputed to be haunted, and as the former occupants have traced the original farmhouse back to 1730, and with the likelihood that the building is in fact older (possibly once housing miners working at Dowber Ghyll lead mines which were opened in 1680), it is difficult to specify the nature of the haunting.

Still with allied aircraft, we come to the phantom Lancaster bomber patrolling the skies around Barnoldswick, less than nine miles as the four-engined heavy bomber flies from Skipton, acknowledged southern 'Gateway to the Dales'. A proliferation of witnesses testify to the sighting in 2004 of an Avro Lancaster bomber, renowned for its role in Operation Chastise, the code name for the 'Dambusters' raid on the Ruhr Valley dams in the Second World War. Manifesting as a low-flying large grey four-propellor aircraft emerging from the mid-morning January mist near to the Rolls Royce factory in the Bankfield area (incidentally the Avro Lancaster was powered by Rolls Royce Merlin engines), the bomber looked set to collide into nearby houses, but vanished before impact. All eyewitness reports agreed that the aircraft was mysteriously silent (the Avro Lancaster was noted for the tremendous roar generated by its four merlin engines), and once reports of sightings came flooding in, this prompted further accounts from other eyewitnesses of a similar Lancaster-type bomber being seen several years previously in the same area. Local knowledge revealed that a small airfield, supposed to have been used as an emergency landing strip during the Second World War, was located at Greenberfield Lane close to the Rolls Royce site. An appeal made by a local newspaper turned up more historical accounts, in particular one gentleman who remembered a Lancaster bomber making an emergency landing close to Greenberfield Lane during the war, with the army and police promptly cordoning off the area to presumably prevent any onlookers from more closely observing the incident.

Other 'ghost planes' have been seen around Yorkshire, supporting the theory of Second World War aircraft silently re-running bombing missions from decades before, breaking through from another dimension. The Sheffield Peaks are rich in sightings of phantom-propelled aircraft and associated ghost airmen, with over fifty planes crashing here during the war. And

The Avro Lancaster bomber.(© Jeremy Stubbs, 2011.)

while it has been suggested that onlookers have mistaken RAF training flights using large propeller-powered Hercules transporters for the Barnoldswick Avro Lancaster, this seems unlikely as the aircraft are marked by distinctive differences (the Hercules' wings are sited higher on the fuselage and the single tail-fin is impossible to mistake for the Lancaster's twin fins). RAF memorial flights in the area have also been proffered as a possible explanations for these sightings, especially over the Bankfield site because of its wartime aviation connections. However, this does not explain the silence noted by all the eyewitnesses, and certainly the RAF would not contravene aviation regulations with regard to low altitude flying (one estimation of the Lancaster's altitude was 400 ft), and especially not over a built-up area.

But the phantom bomber story doesn't end here as two years after the original sightings, a repeat fly past was witnessed in late February 2006, albeit witnessed by only one person in this instance, but headed again in the direction of the Greenberfield Lane strip. So, if you happen to be in the vicinity on a misty winter morning, keep your eyes to the skies and you might be lucky enough to witness a repetition of the flight of one of the most stirring silhouettes of our wartime skies, silently re-enacting an episode from one of the 150,000 missions flown by the Avro Lancaster during the war years.

Finally in this catalogue of the fallen, the appearance of a uniformed First World War solider in the projection box of Ripon's former Palladium Cinema in Kirkgate is somewhat inexplicable. Soldiers had been billeted in the area for some hundred years before the First World War, and prior to the outbreak of hostilities, the town's corporation had already been busy negotiating

Former Palladuim Picture House, now a nightclub.

the establishment of a permanent military training camp as an economy boost for Ripon. The place was therefore well prepared to accommodate what became one of the largest army camps in the country, occupied by some 30,000 soldiers.

The Palladium Picture House as was, built on the site of an old coach house, was converted into a cinema in 1915. Rather poignantly, the Yorkshire Film Archive holds an original 35mm film made by an unknown local cinema owner on Easter Monday, 24 April 1916, entitled 'Scenes from the Ripon Highland Sports', with footage of waving crowds and sporting activities taken during the Highland regiment's day off at Ripon Racecourse. Recovered from the Town Hall and marked for showing at the Palladium in May 1916, sadly many of the soldiers cheer-

ily captured on this film were amongst the regiments mobilised to the front in June and subsequently numbered in the thousands of war dead after the Battle of the Somme which started on 1 July. So perhaps our phantom projectionist's assistant is an imprint left from a happier time, before being claimed by the carnage of one of the Western Front's most tragic battlefields.

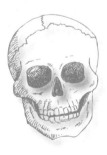

8.

Star-Crossed Spooks

Unlucky in Love

It has long been mooted that the effect of a traumatic event can leave a psychic imprint on the place or location where the experience occurred, hence we have many ghostly accounts connected with extremely strong physical and emotional acts, giving rise to perhaps the favourite of all ghost stories where the recurrent theme sees our phantom crossed in matters of the heart.

Haunting melodies of a lamentable nature are provided by the 'Singing Lady' said to frequent the imaginatively named Cauldron Snout, England's highest waterfall. The eastern end of Cow Green Reservoir, where the River Tees cascades over 200 yds of rock 'stairway', is the chosen spot for the wraith of an unfortunate Victorian farm girl who took her own life in desolation and despair after her love affair with a local lead miner ended. The Singing Lady favours cold, moonlit nights

Cauldron Snout waterfall, haunt of the Singing Lady.

67

and is said to sit on the rocks near the Snout and sing of the loss of her love.

An energetic lover and member of the Ingilby clan (the family associated with Ripley Castle since 1320) kept a number of mistresses dotted around the environs of the ancestral home. His favourite lady was installed at the hamlet of Padside, between Blubberhouses and Pately Bridge and a mere 10 mile jaunt from the family seat. Padside Hall, the stone-built house dating to the late sixteenth and early seventeenth century was an Ingilby property and perhaps presented a convenient venue for covert trysts, but the long suffering Lady Ingilby eventually tracked down and confronted the Padside mistress in the company of her unfaithful husband, presumably in a compromising situation, and cursed them both to a damned and restless afterlife. Within a year, the realisation of Lady Ingilby's words came to pass – her husband virtually decapitated by a low tree branch while out hunting and the mistress carried off by a chill that had worsened to pneumonia. For many years after the double cursing has taken effect, the ghostly vision of a lady and gentleman walking in the Padside area was a frequent sight in the Victorian era, the disconcerted whispering wraiths invariably disappearing into the mist.

Incidentally, leading into the neighbouring hamlet of Thornthwaite (the parish is known as 'Thornthwaite with Padside'), is a road romantically called 'My Love Lane', the junction of this narrow thoroughfare marked with a rough, old-looking small stone block inscribed with 'My Love Lane', and perhaps associated with the cursed lovers frequenting hereabouts on their eternal, tearful wanderings.

Moving on to Giggleswick (although this tale engenders no laughter), neighbouring village to the bustling market town of Settle, a crime passionnel has not only generated a manifestation but has also given name to a bridge. The aptly named 'Beggar's Wife Bridge' is so called as the span was used as the unsuccessful getaway of a fleeing wife running to escape the murderous clutches of her mad, and presumably, penniless husband. Seen re-enacting her flight across the bridge crossing the Tems Beck, a tributary of the Ribble, in a repeated attempt to elude her fate, this is a rather chilling apparition as the lady's facial features are missing, replaced by a spider's web.

From the mere faceless to the entirely headless, we have an example of that most classic of spectral renditions at Rokeby Park, the magnificent Palladian country house built by Sir Thomas Robinson in the 1730s and home to Velázquez's 'Rokeby Venus' (the original now hangs in the National Gallery in London but a copy can be seen hanging in the saloon). Sir Walter Scott was a regular visitor to the house after his friend J.S. Morritt acquired Rokeby in 1769, providing the setting for his epic poem 'Rokeby', incorporating themes inspired by an eighteenth-century legend telling of a former Lord Rokeby of an earlier, unspecified, time who, on discovering his wife's adultery, promptly separated his wife from her head. In an attempt to conceal his crime along with the body, Lord Rokeby submerged his wife's headless corpse at the nearby 'Meeting of the Waters', where the River Greta merges with the Tees. However, his efforts proved fruitless as the wraith of the former Lady Rokeby followed her husband home across the Dairy Bridge to the Mortham Tower, where it is said that drops of her blood dripping from her murderous husband's dagger still indelibly stain the stone stairs. A local parson was called in to exorcise the lady's spirit from the tower, but she didn't go far as her headless form, the train of her long silk dress dragging behind, has been seen on the Dairy Bridge and her piteously wailing entity has also been seen patrolling the riverbank hereabout after dusk.

Another headless lady is responsible for the serious structural alterations made to Rigg House, near Appersett at the upper end of Wensleydale. Former home to one of the Metcalfe clan, a predominant family in this part of Yorkshire and inhabitants of the area since the fourteenth century, known as 'Black Whipper' this particular owner of Rigg House was not well liked. Substantial slave holdings in the West Indies earned him this less than endearing sobriquet, but he was also an unsociable, surly individual. He is said to have shared Rigg House with a woman acknowledged locally as a witch who, after her mysterious disappearance, was blamed for the headless manifestation said to plague her old home. Her haunting was rather vigorous, and held by some as the reason for Metcalfe's eventual quitting of the property – that and the suspicion that he was responsible for the murder. The headless ghost continued to cause serious problems for later occupants of the house until one owner struck upon the smart idea of demolishing the central part of the building most favoured by the ghost. Thankfully this seemed to have the desired effect, the hauntings ceased and this explains why today Rigg House and Rigg House West now exist as two separate dwellings.

The sad tale of the Oughtershaw phantom who evanesces into a puddle of tears on compassionate approach by any concerned passer-by was seen for more than a century after his demise, the result of a

The now separated Rigg House and Rigg House West.

brotherly duel arising from a tragic love triangle back in the sixteenth century. Oughtershaw is one of a group of small villages in Upper Wharfedale strung out along the Oughtershaw Beck, and local gossip concerning Matthew Grigghall's wife and her affair of several years standing with the cuckolded farmer's brother would inevitably reach the wronged husband's ears eventually. To affirm the accusations, Matthew told his wife Rachel he'd be setting off early in the morning to secure the best bargains at Hawes market. After he saddled his pony and set off, unbeknown to Rachel, the suspicious Matthew tethered his mount a mile or so away and surreptitiously returned to his home only to find that malicious gossip was true. To settle the wrong, Matthew challenged his brother Mark to an unconventional duel with pitchforks in an open field at noon the following day. Rumour had it that the vengeful Matthew treated the sharpened tines of his chosen weapon with poison; however, Mark got the better of the fight, landing a blow to his brother's ribs. The now repentant lovers helped Matthew to bed, where he eventually recovered, but as soon as his brother was well enough to run the farm again, Mark left and was never seen again. Seven months later Rachel gave birth to a son, and while a veneer of normal family life was maintained, the living reminder of Rachel's indiscretion was ever present. Some time later Matthew fell seriously ill and, when it appeared that his life was in the balance, Rachel made him swear not to disinherit the boy, in spite of his obviously dubious parentage. Some rumours even inferred that Rachel suffocated her dying husband on his deathbed. In the light of this tragic tale, it was understandably thought that the anguished, wailing soul seen sitting at the wayside was the wraith of the same unfortunate Matthew Grigghall wronged in life and reduced to a pool of lamentable teardrops at the roadside.

The story of a would-be bullying bigamist meeting a sticky end comes to us from the seventeenth-century Braithwaite Hall in the lovely Coverdale, about a mile and a half from East Witton, with its charming stone cottages lining the expansive village green. While the current Hall is the one built by the Purchas family in 1667, there is an earlier reference to a house in 1301 when it was listed as a grange to nearby Jervaulx Abbey, though today luxury bed and breakfast accommodation is offered in an atmosphere of oak panelling and open fires. One can assume that such comforts were not afforded by a former black-hearted Lord of the Manor, referred to only as the 'Big Man of Braithwaite'. Licentious by nature, the bullying Big Man forced his advances on an unwilling village lass named Annie who, despite her fierce attempts to remain in the single state, eventually acquiesced on the grounds that they be married. The Big Man agreed, but unbeknown to Annie the sham ceremony that followed was conducted by a disguised former gamekeeper and therefore had no validity. Annie found herself trapped in a union with a bullying husband, who in order to maintain his wife's compliance imprisoned her sister and kept her hostage at the Hall. Unfortunately, Annie's attempts to release herself and save her sister backfired when, on hearing the key turn in the bedroom one night, in the shadowy flicker of the candlelight she inadvertently stabbed her sister, mistaking her for her boorish husband entering the room. Understandably overwrought, Annie made a dash for it, only to be caught on the road by her husband who was out hunting. Forced to return to Braithwaite Hall, the price of concealing the accidental death of her sister was her continual compliance in the marital bed. However, the announcement of Annie's pregnancy ensured her a temporary respite from the Big Man's unwelcome attentions, and he promptly took a mistress, Sarah, who, after a similar sham wedding ceremony, also believed herself to be the legal wife of the master of the Hall. The Big Man's mistreatment of Sarah was parallel to Annie's sufferings, and not surprisingly the two 'wives' colluded and decided to seek revenge and free themselves at the same time. Over a period of time, the vengeful pair, dosed the Big Man with varying quantities of poison to avoid killing him outright and arousing undue suspicion. Eventually the lethal dose was administered by Sarah (she and Annie had played a game of Chance to decide who would deal the final blow). Some months later Annie gave birth to a son, Thomas, and mother and child lived happily at the hall with 'Auntie' Sarah until Thomas came of age and duly inherited on his twenty-first birthday.

Strangely, though, shortly after Thomas's coming of age, the manor was put up for sale, and mother, son and Sarah left in some haste. There was some suggestion that Thomas had bought a plantation in the Americas, however local gossip laid the reason for their hasty disappearance down to the murder perpetrated some twenty-one years earlier and the reappearance of the Big Man's ghost to his son on the eve of the boy's inheritance. Repeatedly, the wraith of a very tall man would appear to Thomas,

Braithwaite Hall.

standing at the foot of his bed and holding out an empty upturned goblet. The apparition so rattled the boy that he, Annie and Sarah sought to free themselves of ghostly reminders of their past misdeeds by fleeing the house altogether. However, they appear not to have escaped very far, as on cold winters' nights it is said that three hurrying figures can be seen crossing the village green at East Witton. Although, if they thought they could escape the haunting of their former tormentor, they may have been mistaken as sometimes a fourth shadowy figure of exceptionally tall stature is seen to follow.

Another 'big man' with the ubiquitous nickname of 'Tiny' Thwaite was a blacksmith who lived in Gargrave, one of the larger villages set astride the River Aire in the Craven District. Supposedly standing 6.5ft tall in specially made boots and possessing a fearsome temper, Tiny had relocated to the Dales in order to escape Scottish jurisdiction for a brutal murder he had committed back home on the Orkney Isles. He took a shine to the rather accommodating landlady of his local public house, and, in view of her penchant for sharing her charms, coupled with Tiny's disposition for mindless violence, the inhabitants of Gargrave could see trouble coming. Deciding to take matters into their own hands, the cuckolded publican was chosen to heavily dose Tiny's pint with a quantity of digitalis which should have felled an ox. However, the resilient blacksmith merely suffered some stomach pangs and the unfortunate landlord's body was later found with a broken neck. In light of this failure and the landlord's fate, no further attempts were made to eradicate Tiny from the community; however, after the object of his desire ran off with a regimental recruiting sergeant, Tiny never regained his former vigour and his following decline culmi-

nated in what was described in the sixteenth century as an apoplexy. Collapsing by the roadside with no assistance offered, he was carried off in the cold of the winter's night. Laid to rest in unconsecrated ground, in presumably a larger than standard grave cut, Tiny's restless spirit was to intimidate the folk of Gargrave village for at least a century after his death, with pre-dawn door banging violent enough to shake the buildings to their foundations. Eventually Tiny's noisy reign of terror was brought to a close with an exorcism in 1671, and Gargrave today remains free of forceful knocker rattling, although the the Old Swan on the High Street does boast a resident ghost who likes to moves objects around the bar – perhaps Tiny toning down his audible performance in his haunting dotage.

In the shadow of the 'Devil's Bridge' at Kirkby Lonsdale (see 'The Devil's in the Dales' for more about this satanic crossing), two lovers are said to share the same watery fate, foreseen by a renowned local witch called Molly Hall. The tragic chain of events was set into motion one rainy night by a game of cards, when acknowledged local gambler and womaniser Tom Grinton was uncannily dealt the Queen of Hearts six times in a row. Molly correctly predicted that Tom would be dealt the fateful card a seventh time and that this was a warning that a terrible fate would befall Sarah Haygarth, the only woman fool enough to remain faithful to Tom in spite of his philandering and accumulating gambling debts. In the next hand dealt to Tom the red Queen duly appeared, and, somewhat rattled by the turn of events, Tom's guilty conscience drove him to seek out Sarah and reassure himself that the witch's predictions were merely her way of scolding him for his reprehensible behaviour. As frantic knocking on the lady's door solicited no reply, and with Tom now desperate to assure himself of Sarah's safety, he rushed to their secret meeting place below the parapets of Devil's Bridge, hoping to find her there. Repeatedly calling her name, Tom waded out from the shallows thinking he heard Sarah's cry from further out in the swelling river. However, both fates had already been sealed by the cards. Tom slipped on a stone and fell into the torrent, his body recovered the following morning along with that of Sarah who it was ascertained had drowned some several hours before Tom's arrival, having already taken her own life in despair of ever truly attaining his love.

At Mill Gill Force, a hidden treasure of a waterfall is concealed in the strip of wood-land following the gill's path downstream to Mill Gill Bridge on the road to Askrigg in Wensleydale. For many this charming market town will forever be 'Darrowby' after the extremely popular television adaptation of James Herriot's *All Creatures Great and Small* was filmed here. But a far cry from the trials and misadventures of 1940s rural Yorkshire vet, the ritualistic double murder of a young man and woman in the early sixteenth century also took place here, and lends an eerie quality to the location. Leading up from St Oswald's Church along a mile or so of footpath, a ravine is reached where, at the narrowest point, the bodies of the assumed lovers were found with their wrists bound with lengths of their own

The River Lune, flowing beneath the Devil's Bridge, Kirkby Lonsdale.

hacked-off hair. At the time it was deduced from their clothing that the couple were gypsies, and while no charges were brought, a local farmer was suspected of the crime (although the supposition that a gypsy curse was responsible for his curdled milk seems a rather insubstantial motive for murder). However, on closer inspection in what must have passed for an autopsy at the time, it was seen that the cause of death in each case was the gruesome insertion of a pin (or other narrow blade) through the ear and into the brain of both the unfortunate victims. This *modus operandi*, taken into consideration with the fact that the wrists of the victims were bound with their own hair, lends weight to the likelihood that these murders were ritualistic and probably the culmination of a 'blood feud' between opposing Roma families in the area – worthy of a Shakespearean tragedy.

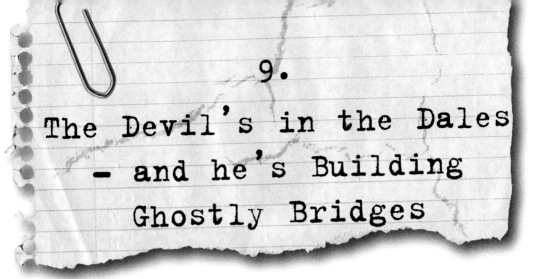

9.
The Devil's in the Dales – and he's Building Ghostly Bridges

WITH his punchbowls, quoits and cheese rings, Old Nick must have been continually busy leaving his mark on the landscape of our British Isles. Where the Yorkshire Dales are concerned, there's no indication of his putting his satanic hooves up; no account of ghostly doings in the district would be complete without a mention of the fantastical, haunted places associated with the mark of the Dark One.

There are a number of 'Devil's Bridges' in the Dales – probably the most notable to be found is at Kirkby Lonsdale. This beautiful triple-arched twelfth-century bridge spans the River Lune, and is now a regular meeting place for motorbike enthusiasts on a Sunday morning (Hell's Angels I hear you ask?). The ghostly legend associated with the bridge involves a woman who had been separated from her cow by the rising River Lune – she is said to have made a pact with the Devil that if he would build a bridge to effect a reunion with her prize milker, in return she would surrender up the soul of the first living thing to cross the bridge. Never one to sniff at the opportunity of acquiring a soul, the Devil obliged, but

the woman tricked her dog into running across the bridge and therefore the disgruntled Prince of Darkness had to make do with the soul of an animal. A bit harsh on the dog (although happier versions tells of the safe return of the woman, dog and cow). This ghostly legend possibly reflects the ancient folk belief in a foundation sacrifice, where in the remote past the offering of a soul when bridges were built would guard against any malevolent river spirits, and serve to protect the bridge against evil, the structure being neither on land nor water. Still to this day, underneath the arches of the bridge can be seen a rock bearing a large, eerie perforation – the 'Devil's Neck Collar' apparently lost when Old Nick discovered his hellish scheme had come to naught.

In Dibbledale, in the valley of the River Dibb, one of England's shortest rivers flows out from Grimwith Reservoir and down under Dibble's Bridge, supposedly built by the Devil in a moment of rare generosity for a local shoemaker who shared a drink with him. There are other diverse local legends concerning Ralph the shoemaker and how the Devil was persuaded to construct

The Devil's Bridge at Kirkby Lonsdale.

Kilgram Bridge minus the mysterious missing stone.

a bridge for his benefit, but all essentially show his satanic majesty in an unusually favourable light. Nearby at Howgil we also find 'The Devil's Apronful', a cairn supposedly the result of a satanic trip-up when, determined to fill up the ravine of the Dibble (or perhaps carrying the foundations for Ralph's bridge), the Devil is thought to have caught his foot on the top of Nursa Knott and, stumbling, dropped the rocks. Spookily, it would appear that the rocks remain in this unusual positioning even today.

Yet another 'Devil's bridge' can be found between Middleham and Masham, where Kilgram Lane crosses over the River Ure. Traditionally marking the lower end of Wensleydale, this ancient span with its mediaeval ribbed arches is believed to have been built in the early twelfth century by Cistercian monks who founded nearby Jervaulx Abbey. Beneath the protection of the bridge lies a former crossing and one of the best preserved paved Roman fords in Britain. However, eerily, legend attributes the construction of Kilgram Bridge to the Devil rather than the Jervaulx brothers, after a pact was made with the local populace, and to this day superstition holds that if the one missing stone in the fabric of the bridge is ever replaced, a satanic curse will fall on the repairer.

The aptly named Hell Gill Bridge, a spooky crossing at Hell Gill Beck, allows walkers to traverse part of this popular route within the Dales National Park. Here the presence of a mound of stones nearby appears to point to local legend that suggests satanic association. According to the legend, the Devil took a pile of rocks from the top of a mountain for use in the construction of the bridge (presumably to keep his hooves dry), his apron strings snapped

and the stones fell to earth. The current Hell Gill Bridge is a single-arched stone span dating from 1825, replacing an earlier structure from which a small stone is still retained and incorporated into one of parapets (thought to be an old boundary stone between Yorkshire and what was then Westmorland).

Tales of a further bridge with demonic associations and resident ghost come to us from Clapham, the peaceful riverside village at the foot of Ingleborough and associated with the ghost of Dame Alice Kyteler, one-time resident of Clapdale Hall in the fourteenth century and supposedly a witch. Four-times married Alice (her previous three husbands had died in mysterious circumstances) became the subject of inquiry when her last husband, Sir John le Poe, succumbed to a wasting disease. Resident in Ireland at the time (Alice held the distinction of being the first person in Ireland to be charged with witchcraft and sorcery), although she was protected initially by her social position and influence, Alice fled to the relative safety of her stepson's house in Clapham, where she remained until her death some years later. Said to drift aimlessly about the Hall, possibly the victim of her own guilty conscience, she may be the same 'White Lady' who has been known to cause a fright at High Clapdale Farm nearby – although her favoured and most dramatic appearance occurs on Clapham Bridge near St James' Church. Here, following a rumoured pact made with the Devil to secure her stepson's unending prosperity, Dame Alice is seen to re-enact a midnight ritual where, standing in the centre of a circle of nine freshly killed red cockerels, she frantically sweeps dust on the bridge in the direction of the Hall, repeating the chant 'Into the house of John, my sonne, Hie all the wealth of Clapham towne'. However much of this story is founded on fact, Dame Alice and her nine dead red cocks are still represented today in the carvings on Clapham's Millennium Stone, featuring aspects of the village's history (located near to St James' Church). From millennium stones to mill stones, ghostly grinding was heard rumbling at Robin Hood's Mill, just below the road from Little Stainforth to Giggleswick for years after the mill was said to have been swallowed into the ground, a punishment meted out to the miller for working on the Sabbath. The site of the mill is now a hollow filled with stones, as over time the weight of the perpetually busy money-making machinery caused the mill to sink further and further into the ground, taking the greedy miller with it.

Old Nick also has a hand in milling local legend from Kirkby Stephen. Here, at Skenkrith Bridge, if one places an ear to the rock, it is thought that you will be able to hear an auditory phenomenon in the form of the low rumbling noise generated by the waters of the River Eden passing over the impressive rock bed formations – thought to be employees of the Devil crushing mustard seeds of all things!

Skirting the edge of the Dales but this time in a southern direction (if only he'd thrown just a little bit harder) and too interesting to dismiss on a point of geographical stricture (Satan was after all supposed to be stood on How Hill when he launched these missiles, so had at least one hoof planted firmly in the Dales), we find the Devil's Arrows, three huge standing stones or menhirs on the western outskirts of Boroughbridge. Thought to originally number five, the fourth stone

was reputedly broken up in 1582 to build the bridge over the River Tutt, and the fifth stone – who knows? Some suggestion has been made that the stones were erected by the Romans to commemorate a great victory (there is a Roman fort immediately west of the stones); however, they are known to date from the late Neolithic or early Bronze Age period. It is believed that the stones were once the site of a solstice fair – several astronomical alignments have been postulated, as well as a connection with a ley line structure. The stones have been known by other names through the ages, variously the Devil's Bolts, the Three Greyhounds and the Three Sisters. The story giving rise to the Arrows epithet seems to date back at least to an account recorded in 1721 when Satan, annoyed by some bad word-of-mouth on the part of the inhabitants of nearby Aldborough, threw the stones at the village from his vantage point on How Hill (south of Fountains Abbey). Either his accuracy or strength failing, the 'arrows' fell short by something of a mile and planted in the earth where they stand today. In a superstitious hark back to the Arrows' satanic origin, it was also claimed that to walk round the stones twelve times withershins (anti-clockwise) will raise the Devil!

We have more ghostly rock in the form of the 'Devil's Stone' on the west-facing slope of Addlebrough Hill near the small town of Bainbridge in the lovely Wensleydale. This huge stone, resting halfway up the slope, is the residue of a row between Lucifer and an unnamed (but unusually friendly) giant who lived on the hill. Determined to gain possession of the giant's crag, a stone-throwing match ensued, the Devil's fingerprints accounting for the

Two of the three remaining menhir stones, or 'Devil's Arrows', at Boroughbridge.

the curious markings left on his boulder (though thought possibly to be cup and ring marks, a form of prehistoric art). For his part, the giant's efforts fell short and landed on the edge of Semerwater, Yorkshire's largest naturally formed lake and rich in its own mythology, and remain on the shore in the shape of the Carlow and Mermaid Stones. These stones too carry another mythology in that they are rumoured to be the site of a druid altar thrown from the top of Addleborough Hill to their current position in a show of strength by the Devil.

Another ominous Devil's Stone, this time located in the unlikely environs of the church of St Michael and All Angels in Copgrove, some six miles south of Ripon,

it was built into the exterior fabric of the north chancel wall. Known locally as the 'Devil Stone', this now badly worn carving (the stone was moved inside to prevent further erosion by the Yorkshire elements) is thought to be of Romano-British origin, and of a type of carving known as a Sheela-na-Gig, figurative depictions of naked women displaying what could be politely described as a gynaecologically exaggerated motif! But you may question why such a carving is associated with a Christian church. There is a theory that many churches were sited on former places of pagan worship; therefore, the incorporation of primitive pagan symbolism into the fabric of a church, smoothing the acceptance of Christianity, is not that unusual.

In the case of the Copgrove stone, one can say with certainty that whatever the carving's origins, she's certainly an exhibitionist!

The Norse equivalent of Satan, the god Loki, is pictorially represented in another church, this time in St Stephen's parish church, Kirkby Stephen, on the beautifully carved 'Loki Stone'. Described as the 'Cathedral of the Dales', of the three successive churches built on this spot, the Saxon predecessor must have been the first edifice to house this relief of the Norse god, a horned figure depicted as bound and chained. Widely accepted as dating from the eighth century, the Loki Stone harks back to the early Viking settlers in the vicinity and the Norse influence before the arrival of Christianity in these parts. The stone itself has been much moved over the centuries and, for many years, was subject to the harsh weathering of the North Yorkshire elements while propped up outside the east end of the church. However, as one of only two known examples of its kind in Europe, the stone's new position inside St Stephen's (directly opposite the main south door) is far more conducive to preserving the detail of this remarkable carving, showing Loki as a bound and vanquished demon. It was possibly adopted by the early church as positive representation of the triumph over evil, and a reminder that Satan in one guise or another has always been prevalent in our ancestral psyche.

The Devil gets another geological look-in at Mother Nature's staggeringly beautiful rock formations at Brimham Rocks, 50 acres of Millstone Grit outcrops carved into strange shapes by the erosion of wind and rain over millenia. Boasting the 'Devil's Anvil' amongst other imaginatively named outcrops, this formation is perhaps

The Copgrove 'Devil Stone'.

The Loki Stone, St Stephen's Parish Church, Kirkby Stephen.

countered by being called 'the Pulpit'. The much visited Brimham Rocks is now in the care of the National Trust and presents something of a geological playground, with uninhibited access for those wanting to enjoy fresh air and splendid views out across Nidderdale.

The Wicked One also appears to have been busy in the culinary sphere, as in the churchyard of St Michael the Archangel in Kirkby Malham; at midnight once a year, he sets out a spectral feast fit for a king, which is said to be an attempt to lure the living to him. Also described as the 'Cathedral of the Dales', clearly vying for the title against the more northerly claimant at Kirkby Stephen, the austerely beautiful fifteenth-century St Michael's, was a parish endowed with a very canny parson named Revd Knowles. It is said that Knowles was the last person to sit down to the lavish devilish banquet, having thwarted the attempt on securing his soul by causing Old Nick to vanish when he asked for some salt, reinforcing the old belief that once, long ago, some salt had been put on the Devil's tail causing severe burns (you'd have thought he'd have been at home with a bit of heat ...) causing him to bite it off to gain relief. So if you come across a Manx Mephistopheles in these parts, don't accept his invitation to a ghostly picnic!

A flavour of the impressive rock formations at Brimham, Nidderdale.

The churchyard of St Michael the Archangel, Kirkby Malham, venue for the Devil's midnight feast.

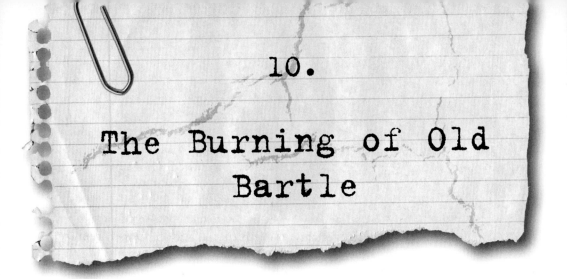

10.

The Burning of Old Bartle

T0 any casual visitor to Wensleydale, or those merely passing through the National Park, the small and unassuming rural village of West Witton on the northern-facing lower slopes of Penhill seems innocuous enough. Another Dales village, Witton is not your archetypal chocolate box tourist honey trap, yet the solid, honest stone houses strung along a narrow main street, set amongst hay meadows and former arable fields, offer charm enough. And at 600ft above sea level perched on the rocky outcrop between the River Ure and widely recognised silhouette of Penhill, the village is the perfect base for some excellent fell walking as well as some equally excellent public houses. There is, however, concealed beneath the surface of everyday Witton life, the secret of a curious – and some would say brutal – ceremony which is annually re-enacted through a sacrificial parade culminating in a fiery crescendo – 'The Burning of Old Bartle'.

A true community occasion, the 'Witton Feast' is a weekend of village events, beginning with the Cottage Show and the popular West Witton Fell Race, run over the upper crags of Penhill. However, this is just the precursor to the real show stopper – a night-time procession of some 200 people following the progress of a gruesome Guy Fawkesesque effigy paraded down the main street before being consigned to a symbolic fiery death. The larger-than-life straw-filled mannequin, with a grisly masked face and light bulbs for eyes, is constructed in secret by a local family some weeks prior to the parade (which is always held on the Saturday nearest 24 August – St Bartholomew's Day.) Carried by two bearers, and accompanied by a stick-wielding 'caller' who repeatedly chants the 'Bartle Doggerel' on the progression through the village, around 9 p.m. Bartle débuts near Kagram's Green Hill at the western end of the village where the merriment and drinking begins. The Doggerel, ritually recited at specified locations where the parade halts en route through the village, is also the point at which the bearers are rewarded with a drink or three :

> On Penhill Crags he tore his rags,
> Hunter's Thorn he blew his horn,
> Cappelbank Stee happened a misfortune
> and brak' his knee,
> Grassgill Beck he brak' his neck,

Wadhams End he couldn't fend
Grassgill End we'll mak' his end

Shout, lads, shout!

Bartle in return brings prosperity wherever he goes, demonstrating a great generosity of spirit in view of the fiery fate repeatedly befalling him year after year in the flaming finale played out at Grassgill End, where the Bartle effigy is anointed with a touch of accelerant and set ablaze to the general delight of the cheering crowd.

It would be a fairly solid assumption among the paranormally minded that the ghost of Old Bartle, after meeting such a violent end, would still frequent any number of the Doggerel locations where he came upon increasing misfortune. And while today a scorched area of dry stone wall serves as a year-long reminder of what has taken place, the origins of the Bartle tradition remain varied and in some instances obscure. However, one certainty is that in spite of the lack of concrete facts for the founding of this custom, the local enthusiasm for this annual event is in no way diminished and it is the definite high point of the Witton calendar.

The most frequently mooted identity for Bartle is that he was a sixteenth-century livestock thief who was caught operating in the area, lynched and despatched in suitably brutal fashion by the good folk of West Witton, who were clearly angered by the illicit purloining of their diminishing flocks. Another candidate is the bad old Giant of Penhill, in local legend an ill-tempered ogre said to utilise the lower slopes of Penhill for his pig farming venture – that is when not tirelessly engaged in terrorising the inhabitants of the village. The Penhill Giant was said to have owned a proportionally large-sized wolfhound called 'Wolf Head', but clearly the dog was an ally of the villagers as belying the normally placid and devoted nature of the breed he is said to have slain his former master while in ghostly form, thankfully ridding the area of this enormous malevolent presence. A further suggestion for the identity of Bartle has been associated with the one-time abbott of Jervaulx Abbey (the Cistercian house linked to the supposed hidden chantry chapel accessed by a secret tunnel at the western end of the village and dealt with more

The blazing effigy of Bartle consumed by the flames at Grassgill End.

fully in 'Ecclesiastic Ectoplasm'). Adam of Sedburgh, whose enforced involvement with the ill-fated Pilgrimage of Grace led to his eventual imprisonment in the Tower and later his execution, fully knew that the anti-Reformation rally was doomed from the start, but the men behind it were insistent that he join their cause. Knowing that his fate would be sealed if he participated with the demonstration against Henry VIII's process of monastic elimination, Adam hid out in the surrounding countryside, but was eventually discovered and physically coerced into joining the cause at Waddam's End in West Witton (the location of his capture and one of the locations mentioned in the Doggerel).

It may be no coincidence that The Burning of Old Bartle always takes place on the Saturday nearest St Bartholomew's Day, this being the saintly dedication of West Witton's church and Bartle being the contracted version of that name. The further possibility exists that The Burning of Old Bartle may have originated as a pagan harvest ritual linked with ancient sacrifice to any one of the pantheon of pre-Christian Sun deities, or the Bartle of today may even be a representation of the Christian wooden statue of St Bartholomew. This was a religious treasure venerated and hidden by the villagers during the Reformation from the ransacking soldiers, who were sent to remove idolatrous images from their local church. The chase played out in the verse may well follow the progress of the villagers on the run with their precious icon, which was subsequently disfigured and finally burnt.

Whatever the true origins of this bizarre tradition, it is clearly very much alive today, with even a marked walk, the 'Bartle Trail', around and above the vil-

lage with embedded mosaics set into the dry stone walls marking Bartle's progress towards his grisly end. And whether or not the spirit of Bartle still haunts West Witton in the traditional sense, his straw-stuffed entity keeps his story well and truly aflame.

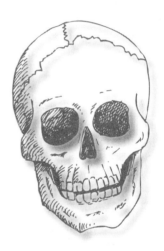

11.

Miscellaneous Manifestations

ERE I have included a selection of hauntings simply too interesting to omit on the basis that they fail to meet the specific criteria of any of the other categories of ghostly tales encompassed in the chapters of this book.

A First Class Phantom

Leyburn Sorting Office, Royal Mail's busy distribution hub for the town and the surrounding rural district, is sited in the former grounds of Thornborough Hall and is home to an elderly gentleman ghost, seen peering through internal fire-door windows and also appearing to a startled cleaning lady. On the morning in question, the cleaner was making her rounds and, knowing that all the staff were out on deliveries, she thought she'd be safe to attend to the gents' lavatory. Her surprise at encountering an elderly gentleman using the convenience was therefore understandable, and after making her apologies for the intrusion and beating a hasty retreat, she mentioned the incident to the sorting office manager. He shared her surprise as he confirmed that there were no staff other than himself left in the building. On later occasions the same 'elderly man' was seen peering through the glass apertures of the internal fire doors. Perhaps this spook was a hangover from the times of Thornborough Hall's heyday, the grounds of which the sorting office now occupies. Today housing local authority offices and Leyburn's library and registry office, the present Hall is made from impressive Victorian sandstone, dating to the 1853 and designed by Joseph Hansom, the York architect and designer of the Hansom cab. Built on the site of an earlier Georgian mansion, fashionable enhancements to the grounds include a 'sham castle' standing at the back of the Hall, and, further along a path, leading to the top of the hill is the hexagonal folly with dramatic views across the Hall's gardens and the town and Dale beyond. Seeming harmless enough, possibly this sorting office spirit is simply availing himself of the amenities in what perhaps appears to be a curious new folly clad in Royal Mail's insignia.

Watery Wraiths

The ghost of 'Ibby Peril' waterfall was noted in Harry Speight's *Craven and the North West Yorkshire Highlands*, published

Royal Mail's Leyburn Sorting Office.

in 1892, where in his 'complete account of the history, scenery and antiquities of that romantic district' she gets a mention in the pages covering Dent. The still cobbled streets of this remote village, the sole settlement in the secluded Dentdale and referred to by locals as Dent Town, is still a strong draw for visitors who come to enjoy the plentiful walks and fine scenery replete throughout this particularly lovely dale. The ghostly witch is said to lurk behind Ibby Peril, or 'Ibbeth' Peril as the waterfall now appears on modern Ordnance Survey maps, a couple of miles east of Dent Town off the Dales Way footpath. 'Ibby' is far more likely to snag a passing canoeist these days as the series of waterfalls on this section of the river Dee prove an active challenge, although her preferred prey is said to be those who inadvertently stray too close, suffering the effects of 'one too many at the bar'. Once kidnapped, you can weather the worst effects of your hangover in her secret dark cave, hidden behind the curtain of falling water.

A most recent addition to the category of waterfall wraith is the image of the ghostly form widely described in the national press as akin to one of the 'Nazgul' Ghost Riders from the big screen adaptation of Tolkien's *Lord Of the Rings* trilogy. Inadvertently captured on camera by a Cambridgeshire couple holidaying in the Dales on a visit to Ingleton Waterfalls, is the image of what appears to be a dark robed figure emerging from the rocks at the bottom of the falls. The outline of the entity highlighted by the splashing water was in no way apparent to the couple at the time of taking the photograph; they afterwards sat down and enjoyed a cup of coffee. The Ingleton Waterfall Walk is a circular trail and offers some of the best waterfall and woodland scenery to be had in the north of England at any time of year through a geologically diverse landscape. However, the town of Ingleton itself is no stranger to macabre goings-on as the spectral sibling rivalry of the two quadrilling Gatenby sisters proves. Tradition has it that in the mid-1600s the two sisters, each intent on solely inheriting their mother's estate which, rather than being equally apportioned, was entailed according to the once popular 'Tontine' law (implemented to prevent the breaking up of a family estates and repeated payments of death duty), poisoned each other in a last-woman-standing 'winner takes all' inheritance race. With their mother barely cold in the ground, the sisters independently both struck on the idea of poisoning one another at the funeral supper; however, their misdeeds were equally repaid when both died within minutes of each other. Ironically, as neither had left a will the property would have passed to the surviving sister, but with the Tontine inheritance law still applying, the subsequent legal wrangle to establish the closest relation (incidentally a distant cousin) swallowed half the value of the estate in lawyers' fees. After their deaths, and in the best tradition of all the good ghost stories, at the stroke of midnight twice weekly on a Wednesday and Saturday, the Gatenby girls would rise from the grave and begin a haunting version of the childhood game of hide and seek, chasing one another around the streets of Ingleton. Once each sister had in turn found the other's hiding place, both returned to the stillness of the churchyard. This bizarre occurrence is said to have troubled the inhabitants of Ingleton for a very specific duration of seven years and seven months, perhaps governed by the fact that this is the exact amount of time it took for their troubled inheritance case to be settled.

School Days

Ermysted's Grammar School in Skipton is an educational establishment of long standing, founded over 500 years ago. Though named for its second benefactor William Ermysted, the original benefactor Peter Toller founded the school in the 1490s. The ever prestigious position of mastership was a distinguished one, and Revd Robert Thomlinson is said to have secured his appointment as a result of a 'smear campaign' mounted against his predecessor Revd Thomas Gartham, whom he ousted in January 1822 and embroiled in a court case the following year. Whatever the methods employed by Thomlinson, if they were underhand then he certainly didn't abide by the school's motto 'Suivez La Raison' roughly translated from the French to mean 'follow the truth'. Rumours were quick to circulate that the death of the fifty-eight-year-old Revd Thomlinson on 28 November 1835 was brought about by the vengeful ghost of Gartham scaring him to death!

Giggleswick School near Settle was established with land granted by the Prior and Convent of Durham in 1507. However, with a view to expansion the school moved from the small building located by St Alkelda's Church up the hill to its current site in 1867. While heard and not seen, the authoritative voice of a former house master is said to echo the corridors after lights out, although rumour has it that his ghostly vocalisations are possibly an invention of the current house masters, employed as a measure to ensure boarders are safely asleep in their dorms.

To more intimate schoolroom surroundings, and that much romantically fictionalised position of Victorian governess, at Kiplin Hall near Scorton (the reader may recall that twenty-five individual hauntings have been so far reported from this Jacobian mansion), the ghost of a grey-haired woman thought to be a governess has been seen in the former schoolroom. Perhaps she was rather strict, as the sound of disembodied sobbing has also been heard and other poltergeist activity at the hall has been attributed to phantom children.

Break a Leg

The Georgian Theatre Royal in Richmond, built in 1788 by actor-manager Samuel Butler, has enjoyed a checkered history as well as being reputedly haunted. When the theatre first opened its doors,

Richmond was the acknowledged fashionable centre of Georgian Swaledale, and with enough salubrious partons to make appearances by Sarah Siddons and Edmund Kean financially viable, the playhouse prospered. However, in time interest eventually waned, and with the declining frequency of performances, by 1830 the Theatre Royal's final curtain came down. In the interim the building was utilised for a variety of purposes (let as an auction room in 1848 with wine vaults constructed in the pit around the same time, and when the theatre was rediscovered it was being used as a furniture store). But with time, love and energetic fund-raising, the Georgian Theatre Royal was restored to its former glory and re-opened in 1963; it is now Britain's most complete Georgian playhouse. But what of its ghost? Apparently the theatre has a strong haunting tradition, with many having felt a

Kiplin Hall, built in the 1620s for George Calvert, first Lord Baltimore and home to a plethora of paranormal presences.

Richmond's Georgian Theatre Royal.

presence over the years, and much publicity given back in 1966 to the experience of the deputy stage manager working on the production of Tate's eighteenth century version of *King Lear*. Working alone in the theatre, the deputy stage manager became aware of a presence heralded by a deathly quiet that seemed to suspend normal activity for a couple of moments before everything returned to normal. While nobody has been able to specifically pin down a reason for the haunting, perhaps the immortal pantomime line 'he's behind you' really holds some truth in this theatrical setting.

Things That go 'Splash' in the Night?

The Ripon Spa Baths seems an unlikely venue for a haunting, but, nevertheless, staff locking up the premises at night have experienced a definite presence in the otherwise empty building. A sudden drop in temperature has been felt and the sound of footsteps and slamming doors have been heard, with dryers being switched on independent of any human hand. The last spa to open in Britain, and the only one in the country to have been opened by a member of the royal family, the pump room was unveiled in 1905 by Princess Henry of Battenberg,

The impressive art nouveau frontage of Ripon Spa Baths.

Queen Victoria's youngest daughter. Edwardian gentry would pay good money to be electrically 'shocked' in one of the immersion baths, or have their systems cleansed by the foul-tasting sulphur water piped four miles from the sulphur springs at Aldfield in sumptuous art nouveau surroundings. Certainly a step up from bathing arrangements funded by Ripon's generous Cathedral Dean, who in 1890 gave £400 (approximately £30,000 in today's money) to build twenty private cubicles by the River Ure so that the Victorian health conscious could bathe with appropriate modesty. And whether the spirit of the spa is a disgruntled bathing belle, or perhaps registering delayed gratification at the failed project to convert the spa baths into luxury flats, Ripon Spa Baths today offers saunas, sunbeds and massage treatments in the Battenberg Health Suite, along with the public swimming pool – no electricity involved!

The pine-covered tumulus of Kirk Carrion, dominating the Lunedale Ridge.

A Hunting We Will Go

Temple Folly, the octagonal Gothic style former hunting lodge built in 1792 and part of the Swinithwaite Estate in Wensleydale, has been beautifully restored from a ruinous state into a weekend hideaway with a balconied turret bedroom much favoured by honeymooning couples. Looking out across the River Ure towards Bolton Castle, Temple Folly, so named as the secluded woodland setting is a stone's throw from the ruined eleventh-century Knights Templar preceptory, is also frequented by the benign ghost of a jolly-looking huntsman, who has appeared to several guests over the years, usually just inside the bedroom door around midnight. Dressed in full hunting regalia, it is assumed that he

is one of the Pilkington family who built nearby Swinithwaite Hall and is continuing the tradition of the building's former use.

Now to a chieftain's tomb where the wind never blows. Seen as a solitary stand of ancient Scots Pines on the Lunedale Ridge some ten miles to the north-west of Barnard Castle, the silhouetted trees mark the site of one of the region's major Bronze Age burial mounds. The tumulus known as Kirk Carrion is thought to be the tomb of the Brigantine prince Caryn, hence the name 'Kirkcarrion', meaning Caryn's Castle. It was constructed sometime around 1400 BC. In 1804 the site was excavated, and the disturbance of the cinerary urn and bones found therein gave rise to the local legends and ghost stories attached to this spot. It is said that

Thorpe Perrow House, perfectly reflected on a calm day.

no matter how rough the weather, within the circle of trees the wind never blows, and when the moon is up the unsettled spirit of Caryn stalks the fells, angry at the desecration of his Celtic resting place. Whatever the truth behind these myths, Kirk Carrion is certainly an atmospheric place, even when visited on a sunny day.

Footsteps and laughter

Thorp Perrow, a gem of Georgian architecture, is gently reflected on the lake separating the house from the surrounding 85-acre arboretum famed as one of the finest private collections of trees and shrubs in the country. Located two miles from Bedale, the creation of one man, Colonel

Sir Leonard Ropner bought the estate in 1927, and very soon afterwards began the planning and planting of the glorious arboretum. Thorp Perrow is still home to Sir John and Lady Ropner, who continue to manage the arboretum which is open to the public all year round, with displays of thousands of daffodils in early spring followed by blossoms through to stunning autumn foliage. The house itself is thought to have been enlarged in 1702 when the two extra wings and ballroom (seen at the front of the house) were added. It is also home to some noisy apparitions, heard by guests and staff with the sound of ubiquitous slamming doors, footsteps, laughter and children playing.

Other titles published by The History Press

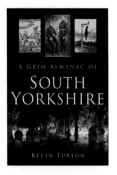

A Grim Almanac of South Yorkshire

KEVIN TURTON

A Grim Almanac of South Yorkshire is a collection of stories from the county's past, some bizarre, some fascinating, some macabre, but all equally absorbing. Within the *Almanac's* pages we visit the dark side, plumb the depths of past despair and peer over the rim of that bottomless chasm where demons lurk, with only a candle's light to see by … metaphorically speaking of course. You are invited to take that journey, if you are brave enough, and meet some of the people that populated the past … while author Kevin Turton holds the candle.

978 0 7524 5678 2

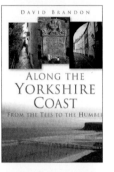

Along the Yorkshire Coast: From the Tees to the Humber

DAVID BRANDON

This book is a unique record of a journey along the beautiful and often dramatic Yorkshire coastline, tracing the region's diverse industry, the history of its settlements, seaside resorts and fishing quays, and reflecting upon the different uses to which man has put the resources where sea and land meet. With a blend of photographs, fact, folklore and social history, David Brandon offers a fascinating and evocative look at the county's local history, and should capture the imagination of everyone who knows the places that are featured.

978 0 7524 5732 1

Curious Tales from West Yorkshire

HOWARD PEACH

This is a charming compendium of historical oddities, curious customs and strange events from across West Yorkshire. Laid out in an easy to use A–Z format, it explores a vast range of subjects, from folklore and legends to Yorkshire's strangest buildings, artefacts and memorials. Here also are some of Yorkshire's most eccentric characters and famous former inhabitants, and the stories behind some of the oddest events that have occurred in the county. Richly illustrated with both modern and archive images, it will delight both residents and visitors.

978 0 7524 5514 3

The Little Book of Yorkshire

GEOFFREY HOWSE

The Little Book of Yorkshire is a funny, fast-paced, fact-packed almanac of the sort of frivolous, fantastic or simply strange information which noone will want to be without. The county's most unusual crimes and punishments, eccentric inhabitants, famous sons and daughters, royal connections and hundreds of wacky facts about Yorkshire's landscape, cities, towns and villages (plus some authentically bizarre bits of historic trivia), come together to make it essential reading and a handy little book for residents and visitors alike.

978 0 7524 5773 4

Visit our website and discover thousands of other History Press books.

www.thehistorypress.co.uk